The Great Memory Book

- ◆ **Boost Confidence & Grades**
- ◆ **Guarantee Your Success**
- ◆ **Discover New Research**
- ◆ **Gain High-Performance Recall**
- ◆ **Learn Practical, Easy-to-Use Tools**

Karen Markowitz
Eric Jensen

CORWIN PRESS
A SAGE Publications Company
Thousand Oaks, California

For information:

Corwin Press
A Sage Publications Company
2455 Teller Road
Thousand Oaks, California 91320
www.corwinpress.com

Sage Publications Ltd.
1 Oliver's Yard
55 City Road
London EC1Y 1SP
United Kingdom

Sage Publications India Pvt. Ltd.
B-42 Panchsheel Enclave
Post Box 4109
New Delhi 110 017 India

Printed in the United States of America.

ISBN: 1-890460-04-4

This book is printed on acid-free paper.

06   07   08   09   10   9   8   7   6   5   4   3   2   1

Memory is the cabinet of imagination,
the treasury of reason,
the registry of conscience,
and the council chamber of thought.

—St. Basil

Contents

Preface

The Great Memory Book is an adventure in learning. You will gain specific practical knowledge as you discover how your memory works and why it sometimes fails. We've included the latest findings in the study of memory to bring you the most complete, up-to-date, and user-friendly guidebook available for developing your full memory potential. Timely topics include memory foods, neuro-nutrients and supplements, exercising your memory, stress effects on memory, fascinating memory phenomenons, strategies for prompting memory, and how to combat age-associated memory decline. To top it off, you will learn all this in a way that sticks: For what is memory if not learning that sticks? When you are done, we guarantee you'll actually *know* the material. You will have experienced it on a deep level. You will have tools at your disposal for remembering whatever you wish. And you can expect to gain self-confidence, improve your work or school performance, and enjoy less recall stress. How is this accomplished? *The Great Memory Book* applies the principles that follow how the brain naturally learns best.

It is not the role of this book to present learning or brain theory, but to incorporate these principles for your benefit. Much like *USA Today, Bottom Line*, or *Reader's Digest,* our intent is to provide the busy reader with the heart and guts of a huge subject in an efficient and effective manner—partly by synthesizing the most pertinent information available on the subject and partly by presenting it in ways that deepen understanding and engage your memory.

Learning that is interactive is better integrated into your memory system; thus, we have included a variety of interactive and brain-friendly features in each chapter. The following "User's Guide" will acquaint you with them and get you started on your *Great Memory* adventure. Our deepest hope is that your explorations into this fascinating realm are as fun for you in the reading as they were for us in the writing. If so, it will be a memorable experience indeed; and memory improvement will be the natural byproduct.

User's Guide

 What's Ahead?: A global overview presented at the beginning of each chapter provides your brain with the necessary connections to interpret the "big picture."

 Case Study: A great deal of research has been conducted in the study of memory over the past few decades. These real-life highlights help engage your emotions and tap into multiple memory pathways.

 Memory P's and Cues: Applications and tips are set off from the text for your immediate implementation. When the brain perceives significance, we pay more attention; thus, we remember it. You might want to copy and post the P's & Cues as simple reminders for yourself.

 **Memory Workout:** These assessment activities provide an opportunity for you to receive feedback on your learning. The brain needs feedback in order to judge and correct its course. The more feedback we get, the faster and more accurate our learning is.

 Memory Booster: These activities (journal exercises and brain games) provide an opportunity to interact with the material, which in turn deepens understanding by engaging your senses and emotions. We are more likely to remember information that we manipulate and think about in various contexts.

 **Recollections:** Each chapter concludes with an interactive synthesis that provides reader feedback, reinforcement, closure, and affirmation of your learning. It also offers an opportunity to see where additional study may be needed.

 **Glossary:** For a brief definition of unfamiliar terms (all capital letters in text), please refer to the glossary on page 189.

Introduction

"I have the worst memory!" At some time or another, we've all been frustrated enough to think that when good memories were being dished out, we missed the boat. But have you ever really stopped to consider what life would be like if you really did have the worst memory—if you couldn't remember *anything* beyond the moment? What if you couldn't recall your own name, your address, your friends and family, how to talk to someone, go shopping, prepare a meal, write a letter, ride a bike, drive, study, work, celebrate, or play? The consequences of having a "bad" memory would be profound; and a life with no memory would be complete chaos.

On the other hand, remembering everything would be equally traumatic. Some things are best forgotten—from the terrible events you wish never happened to the endless stream of trivia you're exposed to daily. It's healthy to forget yesterday's shopping list, last month's travel schedule, and the casual conversation you overheard in the lunchroom. Too much random information makes us crazy—there's no meaning to it. Without the ability to forget, our existence would be like a sleepless night that never ends. You get the idea! We all want to forget certain things and remember other things.

Here's the good news: short of brain damage, there is no such thing as a "bad" memory. Your memory is more likely excellent in some areas and weaker in others. And where it is weak, you can improve it—no matter what your age. By understanding how your memory works you can maximize its power, thereby, improving job performance, school achievement, and personal success. If that's not enough good news, here's more: Exploring the universe within can be one of the most exciting journeys of your life. *The Great Memory Book* is an interactive guidebook to get you started on that journey. Although the subject can be incredibly complex, you're in for a treat. Here, we're breaking new ground with a simple reader-friendly approach to understanding everything about your memory you need to know to optimize its effectiveness.

You'll discover answers to questions like, How can I remember more of what I want to remember? What is extreme memory? Why does a thought sometimes seem to get stuck on the "tip of my tongue"? Where does memory reside? What is Deja vu? Will we someday have access to a memory chip to ensure optimal memory functioning? Why do we forget a person's name only minutes after we hear it? What is "false" memory? How does stress, caffeine, alcohol, and exercise affect my memory? Do the so-called memory enhancers found in health food stores work? Is there really such thing as past-life memories? Why can't I remember much from my early childhood? Why do some memories get repressed? How can I expect my memory to change as I age? If such questions spark your curiosity, *The Great Memory Book* is guaranteed to quench your learning thirst and improve your memory at the same time. May your journey be a fruitful one!

What's Ahead?

Memory Simplified

What Precisely Is Memory?

Memory is the biological process whereby information is coded and retrieved. It is essentially what drives our personality and makes us unique in the animal kingdom. It gives us a reference point for the past and a gauge for the future. Contrary to our collective notion of a personal "memory bank" or storage unit reserved for this purpose, memory, unlike our heart or lungs, is not a singular place or thing. Rather, it is a collection of complex electrochemical responses activated through multiple sensory channels and stored in unique and elaborate neuronal networks throughout the brain. Dynamic in nature, your memory is continually changing and evolving as new information is added to it. With the help of today's technology, scientists have made great strides toward mapping this extraordinarily complex process we call memory.

To develop our memory it is vital that we understand what it actually is and how it works. We'll begin by exploring some common delineations of memory types. Have you ever noticed that some things are easier to remember than others? This is because most of us have a mixture of memory-type strengths and weaknesses. Because different types of memory are stored in various function-specific areas of the brain, the act of recalling something pulls bits and pieces of "memory" together from their respective storage sites. The particular "pathway" accessed in the formation of a memory depends on multiple factors, including time, importance, purpose, content, strength, and the source of the stimuli—the basis of all memory. Each of these factors influences the quality and accessibility of your memory.

■ Types of Memory

The simplest classification of memory is related to life span or memory duration—for example, short-term or long-term memory. The memory duration classification also uses the terms immediate perceptual memory and working memory. *Immediate perceptual memory* lasts less than one second—long enough, for example, to interpret a string of single frame images as a moving picture or a word long enough to type it. *Working memory*, also called short-term memory, lasts long enough, for example, to dial a telephone number you just looked up or to determine how much change you should get in a sales transaction. *Short-term memory* can maintain information for up to twenty seconds, or longer if it is cued or consciously rehearsed. The location of your parked car, for example, can be maintained in short-term memory longer than the standard twenty seconds by noticing obvious landmarks which act as retrieval cues. Information that is encoded in *Long-term memory* can stay vital for up to a lifetime. The ninety-year-old who remembers the day she met her spouse as clearly as if it happened yesterday, displays the incredible duration and power of long-term memory.

Psychologists usually define short-term memory as lasting up to 20 seconds or longer if consciously rehearsed. Most people's short-term memory capacity is limited to remembering seven chunks of information at a time. You are using your short-term or working memory when you repeat a phone number encoding it long enough to dial the correct number.

Long-term memory, which can last up to a lifetime, is kept vital by looking at old photographs or anything that activates your recall; i.e. What do you remember about high school?

Another simple classification delineates memory by the manner in which it is encoded and retrieved—either consciously or instinctually. As such, memory is either *Explicit* (also called declarative) meaning it is achieved through purpose and effort, or *Implicit* (also called nondeclarative) meaning it is arrived at organically or automatically. An explicit memory function, like learning how to spell, requires attention, focus, and practice to remember. Most learning assigned in school is explicit. Implicit memory, like knowing fire burns, on the other hand, represents our most primal memory which helps keep us safe, and ensures our survival as a species.

Four subtypes of implicit memory: procedural, reflexive, sensory conditioning, and emotional; and two explicit memory subtypes: semantic, and episodic, further explain the various functions of memory. Flashbulb memory is best described as a combination of both explicit and implicit memory types (see figure 1.2).

Procedural memory (also known as motor memory) involves learned tasks or skills like fishing, riding a bike, driving a car, or tying our shoe laces. This implicit memory represents the *how to* of a memory task. Though procedural memory is embedded through practice, the skill becomes virtually automated over time. When you jump on a bicycle, for example, you don't have to think about how to ride it. The memory for this skill is automatic.

Procedural memory involves task-related memory acquired by practicing a skill, like driving a car. What abilities do you possess that require procedural memory?

Reflexive memory (also known as stimulus-response) is basic to human survival. This implicit memory pathway codes, stores, and retrieves information instantly and instinctually. One of its primary functions is to keep us out of harm's way as evidenced by the inclination to pull your hand away from a hot stove or to yell "Ahhh!" when someone shoves a snake in your face. The intense combination of a frightening sight, harsh sound, and strong emotion can embed a reflexive memory for a lifetime. Such an experience can seed

Reflexive memory is embedded by intense sensory stimulation. Like the fear of snakes, real or imagined, it can last a lifetime. What are you afraid of?

phobias and persistent illogical fears for a lifetime. This is also the memory pathway that processes intense sensory memory when a smell, sight, taste, song, etc. triggers a core sensation. For example, the smell of a home in which chicken soup is simmering on the stove always reminds me of my Mother's cure for the common cold, depression, or any other ailment known to humankind; and an automatic comfort level is immediately triggered. Though reflexive memory is most often formed unconsciously, we can consciously instill it through repetition or drilling illustrated by the flashcard method of learning. Any procedure that is repeated often enough can become reflexive. A professional baseball player doesn't have time to analyze a fast-ball before swinging; rather, the zillions of previous attempts at the task have reinforced the player's reflexive memory. Likewise, reaching out to shake someone's hand is a reflexive action. The following three subtypes of reflexive memory are often referenced by the following names: flashbulb, sensory conditioning, and emotional memory.

Sensory memory involves the retention of information cued by a particular sense. What memories come to your mind upon encountering the scent of salty sea air?

Sensory conditioning involves the particular sense pathway the memory travels to the brain. For example, visual memory is perceived through the eyes and is stored as concrete images in the visual cortex. As such, it is best retrieved by visual cues or imagery such as pictures, objects, symbols, places, faces, and information on a page. An example of visual memory would be the recollection of your beloved childhood pet when you see that same breed. Auditory/verbal memory, which is stored in the auditory cortex, is best retrieved by cues such as rhymes, jingles, puns, acrostics, acronyms, and verbal associations. The rhyme, "i" before "e" except after... what letter? illustrates your auditory/verbal sensory conditioning; and the associations you make when you breathe in the scent of salty sea air reflects the power of your olfactory memory.

Emotional memory refers to information stored in the brain as a result of intense sensory stimulation. From trauma to pleasure, this direct pathway can produce fast learning.

The following two explicit memory subtypes—semantic and episodic memory—represent most of the learning tasks assigned in school and the learning we gain as well as from life events and experiences.

Semantic memory includes most academic and professional knowledge—ideas, facts, typical exam questions, as well as names, dates, identification numbers, movies, books, pictures, videos, and technical information. The weakest of our retrieval systems, semantic memory, evolved relatively recently. This type of memory, triggered by language and association, was not necessary until

Semantic memory involves the retention of facts and ideas; i.e., Do you remember the names of the planets in our solar system?

recent history when books, schools, literacy, and social mobility became important.

Episodic memory (also known as autobiographical) is driven by location and circumstances. Using the context of the memory as a prompt, we reactivate it. Responding to the question, what did you do during the holidays, for example, prompts your episodic recall. Almost as if a film is rolling, related events, activities, feelings, faces, and places emerge and congeal to form the memory. Native peoples from many parts of the world have relied on storytelling to transmit their history and values to the next generation—an activity that relies heavily on episodic memory.

Episodic memory involves the retention of related time periods, places, and circumstances; i.e., What do you remember about your wedding day?

Flashbulb memory refers to the vivid recollection of an extremely emotional or shocking event, usually captured in the minds of many people—for example, the Challenger explosion or a severe natural disaster. The event is stored with vivid imagery as if it were a moment frozen in time. Although, memories that engage our emotions generally remain potent over time, long-term studies suggest that the details fade in accuracy.

■ *A Multitude of Memory Types*

To "bring home" the various classifications of memory noted above, consider one morning in the life of a fictional character, Jesse. Jesse is awakened with the sun shining in his window which tells him it is past his usual rising time (Implicit, Visual Memory). He jumps out of bed when he realizes his alarm clock has failed (Reflexive Memory). Intending to report the power outage, he finds the power company's phone number and repeats it a few times before dialing (Semantic, Short-Term "Working Memory"). Since he is going to be late for work, he calls his office number which he knows by heart (Semantic, Long-Term Memory). He tries to visualize his calendar to recall if he will be missing any appointments (Explicit, Visual Memory). Jesse does not usually have to stop and think about how to prepare his morning coffee (Implicit, Procedural Memory); however, since today poses a power problem, he can't use the electric coffee-maker. He recalls that he bought instant coffee for his

Smell is a potent wizard that transports us across thousands of miles and all the years we have lived.
—Helen Keller

camping trip last week (Episodic Memory), reminding him that his stove is powered by gas, not electricity (Semantic Memory). Jesse fills a tea pot with water and puts it on the stove. When he hears it boiling, he reaches for the pot, but retracts his hand immediately before getting burned (Reflexive, Stimulus-Response Memory). He dresses quickly and drives to work (Implicit, Procedural Memory). At the office, he remembers that he is expected to provide the board of directors with a summary of the company's annual audit that afternoon. Jesse reads over the report and creates an outline to remember it (Explicit, Semantic Memory). He recalls the President of the company saying that the most critical information in the report is the "the company's unusually high rate of growth" (Semantic, Auditory/Verbal Memory). He makes a "mental note" (cues his memory) to close his presentation with this observation. It is only 10 a.m. and Jesse has already used a multitude of memory types.

Figure 1.1

How Memories Are Formed

1. We think, feel, move and experience life (sensory stimulation)

2. All experiences are registered in the brain

3. They are prioritized by value, meaning, and usefullness by brain structures and processes

4. Many individual NEURONS are acitivated

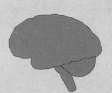

5. Neurons transmit information to other neurons via electrical and chemical reactions

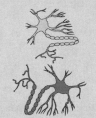

6. These connections are strengthened by repetition, rest, and emotions. Lasting memories are formed.

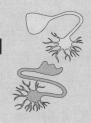

Figure 1.2

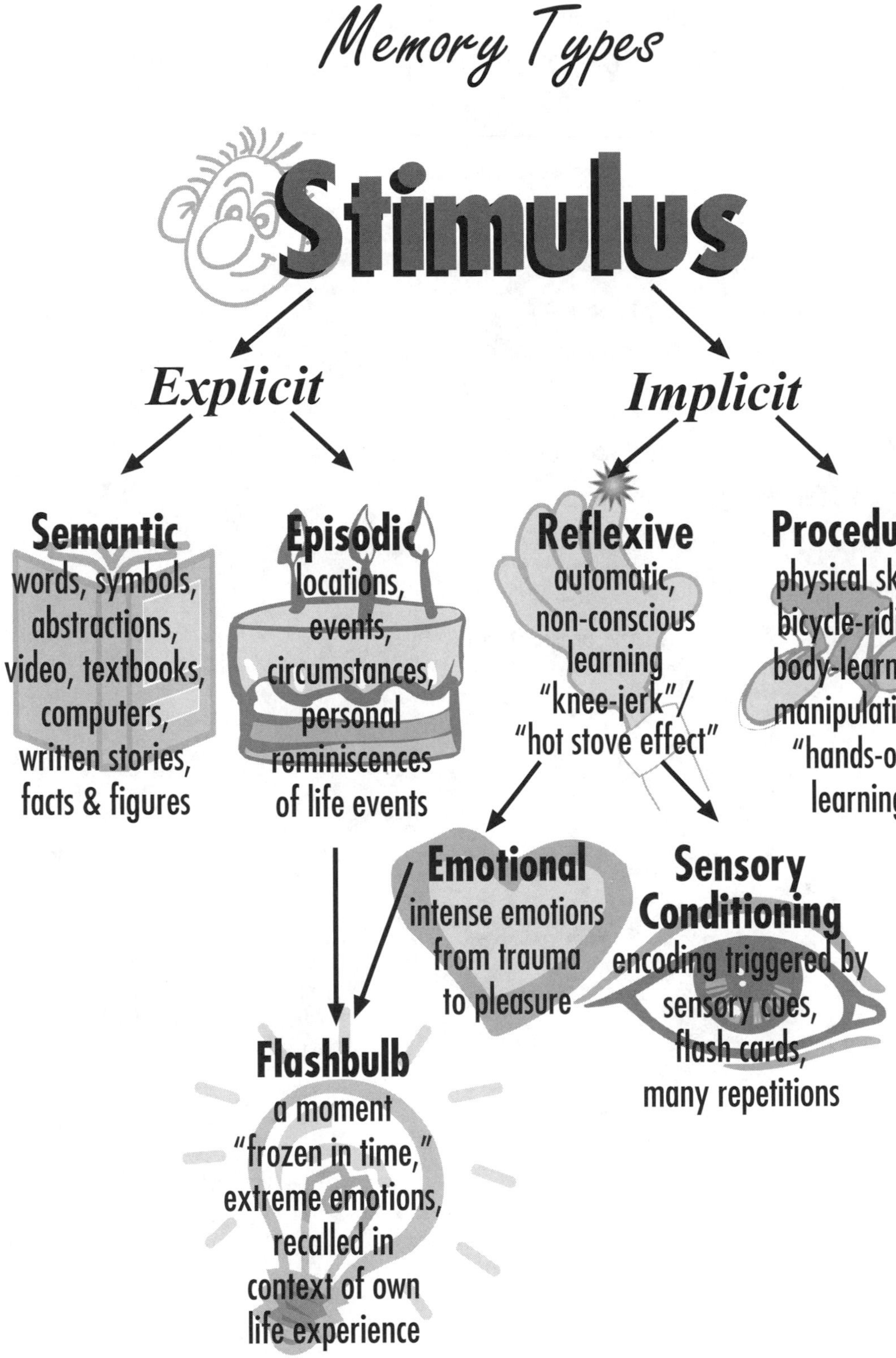

Memory Types

Stimulus

Explicit

Implicit

Semantic
words, symbols,
abstractions,
video, textbooks,
computers,
written stories,
facts & figures

Episodic
locations,
events,
circumstances,
personal
reminiscences
of life events

Reflexive
automatic,
non-conscious
learning
"knee-jerk"/
"hot stove effect"

Procedural
physical skills,
bicycle-riding,
body-learning,
manipulatives,
"hands-on"
learning

Emotional
intense emotions
from trauma
to pleasure

**Sensory
Conditioning**
encoding triggered by
sensory cues,
flash cards,
many repetitions

Flashbulb
a moment
"frozen in time,"
extreme emotions,
recalled in
context of own
life experience

Figure 1.3

Anatomy of a Memory

- Memories are formed when brain cells make connections at the SYNAPSE.
- The process used to transmit information, starting at a cell body, is electrical to chemical to electrical.
- Memories are likely encoded in DNA's sister molecule, messenger RNAs.
- When signals travel across a synapse, mRNAs transmit the information needed to alter the connection.
- As a result, alterations of synaptic strength occur, increasing the probability of future neuronal firings.
- Memory is the increased probability of a particular synaptic firing pattern within a neural network.
- Many neurons are involved in memory formation.
- Neurons that fire together, "wire together."
- Complex memories are based on the binding together of many elements within a network.
- There is no one place in the brain for all memories.
- Explicit memory is more malleable; implicit memory is more fixed.

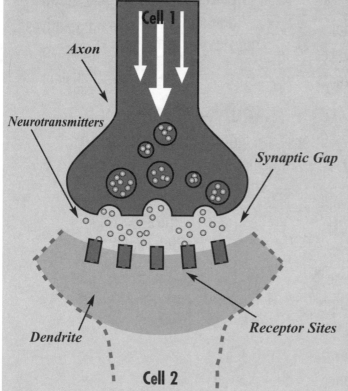

Cell 1

Axon

Neurotransmitters

Synaptic Gap

Dendrite

Receptor Sites

Cell 2

1. When stimulated, electrical impulses travel from the cell body down the axon of the presynaptic neuron.

2. Brain chemicals (NEUROTRANS-MITTERS) are released into the synaptic gap.

3. The receptors on the receiving surface of another cell (the post-synaptic neuron) are stimulated and altered. Encoding is complete.

*H*ow Are Memories Made?

Although most of us have made or heard remarks about how "bad" our memory is, the truth is your memory operates on a continuum of strengths and weaknesses. Much like the concept of multiple intelligences where a person may be a great writer but lack an affinity for math concepts, we can exhibit great strength, for instance, in remembering faces but not where we left our keys. The first step towards improving your memory is realizing what aspects of it are troublesome. Since memories are stored along multiple neural pathways, it is clearly beneficial to understand how a memory is encoded, stored, and retrieved. Once you understand the basic operating principles underlying the memory process, you can outsmart it. Chapters 3 through 5 are devoted to strategies for maximizing your memory. But first, let's take a closer look at the way a memory is made.

■ *A Day In the Life of a Memory*

Even as you read this, your brain is sorting out an astounding mass of information taken in by your eyes, mouth, ears, skin, and nose. Once this stimuli enters your brain through your senses, it is promptly processed by a complex network of neurons, proteins, and electrical impulses. The input of these words on this page, for instance, are now traveling along your optic nerve guided toward their eventual storage destination—your visual cortex within the OCCIPITAL LOBE. If the information, however, does not receive sufficient attention or if it is not deemed necessary for the long-term, it will be encoded for short-term use only and ultimately discarded unless reclassified. The encoding process takes into consideration the emotional nature, value, and meaningfulness of the information, as well as how it relates to prior learning, and how much attention the data has been prescribed. When an experience is recalled, the various elements of it are instantaneously retrieved from their relative storage areas in the brain (*see figure 1.5*) to form an integrated composition which, ultimately, constitutes your memory.

With the advent of positron emission tomography (PET) scans and other neuro-imaging devices, scientists have been able to identify the areas of the brain that process

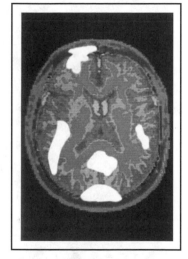

Scientists, using neuro-imaging devices like PET scans, can observe what areas of the brain are activated during specific task-related functions. For example, when a person is reading a book, a PET scan shows activity in the temporal and parietal lobes with some in the occipital, as illustrated by the white areas in the image.

various functional aspects of memory. Consider the question, what did you have for dinner last night? You probably located a clue to stimulate your recall—possibly the particular circumstances or context, for example, surrounding that general time of day: Oh yes, I was home alone last night. A series of cues then stimulate the various elements of the memory in a chain-like fashion: I considered going out for sushi but then I decided I would rather finish reading my novel, so I settled on leftovers from the night before. Your memory of the experience may include a restimulation of the senses involved. It may be prompted by a surprising or novel aspect of the experience or by the company with whom you shared it. These clues or prompts when used consciously are called cues. Improving your memory is greatly dependent upon your effective use of retrieval cues.

Figure 1.4

Cellular Memory Pathway

Activation Here

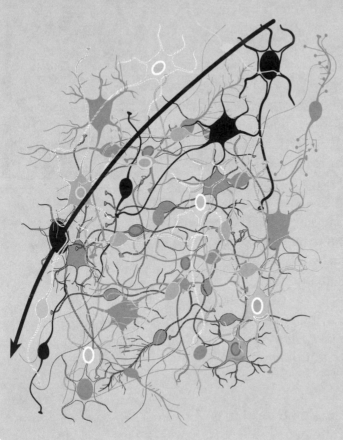

This illustration represents a complex web of NEURONS. Remembering something requires the activation of specific networks of neurons to trigger the exact memory. The darkened neurons are the ones activated. Others remain dormant unless stimulated. The activation of a memory can be triggered by any incoming stimuli on a random basis, or it can be consciously cued into your memory with a MNEMONIC or purposeful memory strategy.

■ *Encoding a Memory*

The first two elements of memory formation—encoding and storage—are essential to the third element of memory—retrieval. If the encoding and storage process is faulty, retrieval is not likely. Thus, we begin to see the importance of these early stages of memory formation. Since memories are stored in a web-like fashion throughout the brain depending on their coding (*see figure 1.4*), it follows that you can improve your memory by learning to encode consciously what you want to remember. This is the basis of mnemonics—the collection of strategies known to aid memory.

For a brief definition of terms marked by all capital letters, please refer to the glossary in the appendix.

You can start to get in touch with your own innate memory abilities by working through the Short-Term Memory Quiz on the following page.

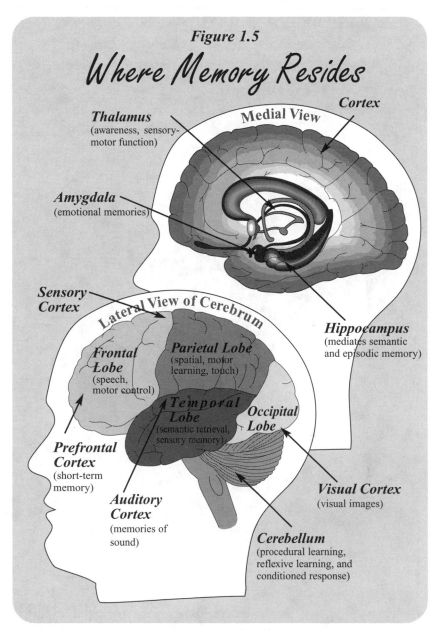

Figure 1.5

Where Memory Resides

Medial View

Thalamus
(awareness, sensory-motor function)

Cortex

Amygdala
(emotional memories)

Sensory Cortex

Lateral View of Cerebrum

Hippocampus
(mediates semantic and episodic memory)

Frontal Lobe
(speech, motor control)

Parietal Lobe
(spatial, motor learning, touch)

Temporal Lobe
(semantic retrieval, sensory memory)

Occipital Lobe

Prefrontal Cortex
(short-term memory)

Auditory Cortex
(memories of sound)

Visual Cortex
(visual images)

Cerebellum
(procedural learning, reflexive learning, and conditioned response)

Bits and pieces of an experience are stored in the various functional areas of your brain. Memories of how something appears, for example, are stored in the visual cortex, and memories of how something sounds are stored in the auditory cortex. Each aspect of the memory is linked to the other.

Memory Workout
Short-Term Memory Quiz

Below you will find a photograph of fifteen everyday objects. Examine the picture for sixty seconds, then close the book and write down as many of the objects as you can recall. After you've completed the first part of this exercise, see page 13 for the second step.

Memory Quiz Answers

Items pictured were:

1. *Plant*
2. *Photograph*
3. *Leaf*
4. *Cup*
5. *Spoon*
6. *Watch*
7. *Computer Disc*
8. *Pen*
9. *Toothbrush*
10. *Tape*
11. *Keys*
12. *Fan*
13. *Water Bottle*
14. *Sunglasses*
15. *Scissors*

Most people are able to recall about eight to twelve of the items correctly immediately following the sixty-second examination period. If you remembered all fifteen items shown, the good news is you may be using a memory strategy (consciously or unconsciously) already. If, however, your memory did not perform as well as you would like it to, apply the following simple association strategy the second time around and see what happens:

How to Recall All 15 Items

There are many retrieval strategies. This one is based on the principles of imagery and linking. When you examine the photograph this time, invent a story in your mind to associate or relate the items to each other. Visualize a scene that puts the objects in a context that is meaningful to you, even though it is artificial. If, for example, I want to remember the following ten words: cup, table, planet, fork, lamp, chair, radio, playing cards, castle, and money-tree, I might visualize myself sitting in a *chair* at the breakfast *table* with a *cup* of orange juice and a *fork* to eat my eggs while I study for a test on the *planets*, but the *radio* is disturbing me so I turn it off and turn the *lamp* on so I can see better, at which time I notice the *playing cards* left out from the previous night's Blackjack session. This triggers my thinking that if I want to build my *castle* in the sky, studying will pay better *dividends* (money tree) than gambling over the long run. There are many variations on the story-technique for memory association; such as, associating by groupings or pairings or by related subjects or letters—whether abstract or concrete, real or made up—studies have shown a marked increase in task-related memory when subjects use association techniques to prompt recall.

Why Do We Forget?

The flip-side of remembering—forgetting—is a universal phenomenon, a biological check and balance that helps us maintain our equilibrium in an otherwise overwhelming world of sensory stimulation. As such, it is not necessarily bad to forget but merely a discrimination function between what is important and what's not. Thus, forgetting is only unfavorable when it involves information that we wanted or needed to remember. When you forget something you want to remember, it is probably due to one of the following factors:

■ *Insignificance*

A perception of insignificance is the most common cause of forgetfulness. Sigmund Freud remarked, "We remember the things that interest us." We all know kids who exhibit great memory when it comes to talking about their favorite sports team or movie star. In the encoding process, much consideration is paid to the relevancy of the information. Quite simply, if information is not deemed meaningful, it will not be stored in long-term memory.

■ *Interference*

Another factor in forgetting is interference—an untimely interruption of competing stimuli during the memory processing stage. When interference occurs, an attempt at memory retrieval will likely be unsuccessful. To experience the effect of interference look up a telephone number you don't know, repeat it a couple of times to store it in short-term memory, and then have a brief conversation with someone. Do you remember the phone number after this? Probably not. Interference can also result in a "tip-of-the-tongue" experience. You "almost" remember something, but it is temporarily inaccessible (more on interference in Chapter 8; more on tip-of-the-tongue phenomenon in Chapter 2).

■ *Deterioration*

One of the oldest explanations of forgetting—the "use it or lose it" theory—suggests that the engram or neural connection that occurs the moment an event is recorded in the mind may deteriorate with time if not "exercised." Exercising the memory trace can be as simple as looking at old photographs, reviewing a story, attending a reunion, reexperiencing a piece of music, or visualizing a scene in your imagination. Though deterioration may be a partial explanation for memory decline in the elderly, much research has shown that a person's memory can be improved long into their senior years with the aid of simple memory strategies. Thus, deteriorating memory does not have to be our fate as we age (more on deterioration in Chapter 8).

■ Repression

Memory repression, whereby a memory is pushed out of the conscious mind, is likely a built-in self-defense mechanism that helps us survive emotional trauma. The theory of repression, first described by Sigmund Freud, explains why some people may remember very little about an extremely distressing event or traumatic period of time. Repression is controversial in nature because memory is malleable and, as such, may be influenced, corrupted, or recalled inaccurately. This is particularly troublesome in court cases that rely on a witness's memory of a situation which may have occurred many years previously. Inappropriate psychological and hypnotic techniques have been used (intentionally or unintentionally) to evoke "lost" memories, sometimes resulting in false memory. Unethical practices by some therapists should not invalidate, however, the help a person may receive from a qualified professional therapist or psychologist in dealing with repressed memories (more on memory repression in Chapter 8).

We remember that which interests us.

—Sigmund Freud

■ Stress

Memory performance peaks with moderate stress. It, however, declines when the stress is excessive or chronic. Since a critical aspect of remembering something is attention and focus, consider what happens to your concentration when you are anxious. In such a state, you are quite likely to make a mistake, forget something, or feel confused. On a physiological level, stress triggers a hormone called CORTISOL which gives you a rush of energy but ultimately inhibits accurate recall over time. Thus, chronic stress is bad for memory (more on stress in Chapters 7 and 8).

■ Retrieval Cues

When we forget something or have a temporary memory lapse, the problem may be in the retrieval loop rather than in the recording process. The memory is there: It just has to be accessed. Once an appropriate cue or association is located, the memory is activated. Consider this simple example: Have you ever walked into the kitchen to get something only to discover that you forgot what you came for? Then, upon returning to your previous setting, your recall is magically restored! It may feel like you're losing your mind, but in reality, you've only lost your memory cue. Something as simple, however, as going back to your office and seeing the empty coffee cup or unopened package on your desk can "jog" your memory (retrieval cue). Once you learn how, you can give yourself conscious memory cues, rather than relying on your unconscious to do all the work. You can, in fact, consciously "cue up," anything you wish to remember, as you'll see in Chapters 3, 4, and 5.

■ *Physical Impairment*

Although there are some serious diseases and mental impairments that adversely affect memory functioning: amnesia, encephalitis (brain swelling), Korsakoff's syndrome (due to alcohol abuse), Alzheimer's disease, and head injuries, relatively few people are impacted by these disorders. It is increasingly recognized, however, that memory functioning is strongly impacted by psycho-social issues like depression, grief, and chronic anxiety.

We Remember...

- ■ **Information that aids our survival**
- ■ **What we give our attention to**
- ■ **What we find meaningful**
- ■ **What we practice**
- ■ **What we link to prior learning**
- ■ **What we encode with a mnemonic or other memory device**

We Forget...

- ■ **That which is insignificant to us**
- ■ **When we are not engaged**
- ■ **What we don't practice, review, or use**
- ■ **When something is too painful to remember**
- ■ **When prolonged stress interferes with brain functioning**
- ■ **When we don't consciously activate a memory cue**

*C*an My Memory Be Improved?

The human brain perceives and processes an astounding quantity of sensory information fueled by about 100 billion NEURONS that have the capacity to make trillions of cellular connections. It is these cellular connections building on one another that activate learning, consciousness, intelligence, and memory. Like a snowball gathering speed and density as it travels downhill, your memory grows exponentially with use, and is highly unlikely to ever reach full capacity. The more learning you do, the more associations your memory can grab onto. You are unconsciously improving your memory every moment that you are alive. The degree of memory enhancement you can achieve by learning about your memory and memory strategies is profound.

Memory Booster

Befriend Your Memory

Begin keeping a Memory Journal. Record things about your memory that you find interesting, frustrating, or surprising. Note the type of memory it is when you forget something. Also record the times when it's served you well — especially when you have applied a retrieval cue that worked. If a cue didn't work, why do you suspect this is? Describe any tip-of-the-tongue experiences, mental blocks, or deja vu feelings that occur. Note any life circumstances that may be affecting your memory (i.e., high stress, a change in diet, vivid dreaming, illness, family death, medications, etc.). Over the next month, write in your memory journal daily, if possible.

Some strategies for remembering to write in your Memory Journal:

- *Leave the journal under your pillow, by the coffee-maker, on the bathroom sink, or other area you use daily.*
- *Post a sticky note on your bathroom mirror.*
- *Carry your journal in your car, backpack, or briefcase.*
- *Visualize yourself writing in your journal at a particular place that you go daily (i.e., work, school, or the gym) or at a particular time (i.e., coffee break, lunchtime, or after the nightly news).*

Use your journal to objectively record your memory experiences rather than to judge them. Getting familiar with your memory, like getting familiar with your computer, arms you with information necessary to maximize its power. As you begin to recognize your strengths and weaknesses, you can apply any number of simple strategies outlined in *The Great Memory Book* to gain greater memory command and self-confidence.

A few basic memory principles, once learned and applied, can help a person remember almost anything. In this sense, your memory capacity is only limited by your perception of its ability. As you begin to work with the memory strategies in *The Great Memory Book*, you will become aware of your own distinct preferences, organizational techniques, concentration abilities, and attention patterns that clearly impact your memory. Though certainly some people have a natural gift for remembering, in general, most people who exhibit an excellent memory have *learned* to remember. And there is more good news—it doesn't take years of practice or an exceptional IQ. We can all, no matter what our age or education level, improve our memory.

■ *Your Memory Modality Preference*

Once you begin writing in your memory journal, perhaps you'll notice that the information you seem to have the most trouble remembering is that which you hear. Or maybe, it is that which you see or do. Most people have a preferred modality for receiving information which, if recognized and applied, will aid their memory significantly. The majority of Americans exhibit primarily a visual preference, whereby, pictures, faces, structures, objects, maps, and words on a page, for example, have more impact on their memory than verbal instructions or sounds. Visual learners prefer to process information with pictures, photos, symbols, outlines, or mind-maps. Auditory learners, on the other hand, prefer to process information with their ears; and find most helpful memory cues linked to rhymes, mottos, jingles, songs, acrostics, and puns. We are all kinesthetic learners, which means we remember best by doing, feeling, or experiencing something in concrete form.

How a person organizes their memory, much like how their office is organized, will determine how efficient their memory system is. Even though a memory may be stored in your mental filing cabinet, you need the "file name" or prompt to retrieve it.

Information that is personally meaningful to you or emotionally laden will be easier to remember than information that is inconsequential or insignificant. For this reason, whole words are easier to understand than a series of meaningless syllables; a sentence is easier to remember than a series of unrelated words; and information experienced in a sensory rich or real-life setting will be more meaningful than that garnered from a book or traditional classroom lesson. It is in this vein that attaching the letters of the alphabet to a familiar jingle like *Twinkle, Twinkle Little Star*, for instance, helps children remember the alphabet, or taking a trip to the zoo helps a child learn about animals.

■ *Seven Basic Memory Principles*

1
Personal Relevance
Is what you want to remember personally meaningful? If not, can you make it so?

2
Concentration
Have you clearly focused on the information you want to remember? The more attention you prescribe it, the stronger will be the memory trace.

3
Multi-Sensory Perception
Have you imagined or visualized what you want to remember? Have you talked about it, manipulate it, or associate a feeling to encode it?

4 State-Dependence

Is it possible for you to match your state of learning when you need to recall the information? For example, if you study for an exam under the mild influence of caffeine, you will best remember it in the same state.

5 Mnemonics

Have you applied a memory strategy to the information you want to remember? There are countless possibilities, as you will discover in Chapters 3 through 5.

6 Mood or Attitude

Are you in a conducive state of mind for learning—free of intense stress, depression, anxiety, or fear? Do you have an "I can do" attitude?

7 Mental Organization

Are you aware of your natural inclinations or preferred modalities for processing, organizing, storing, and retrieving information? Do you consciously encode that which you want to be sure to recall?

Case Study
The Man Who Could Not Forget

Imagine for a moment that your memory is so indelible you can still clearly recall your Mother's face coming into focus as she begins to nurse you. Your sensory perception is so sharp that voices produce colors and vivid images; and numbers represent a symphony of sights, sounds, tastes, smells, and feelings. You are able to repeat multiple lists of seventy numbers read to you, not only forward, but backwards; not only an hour after the list is heard, but fifteen years later, as well. This was the real-life experience of Solomon Shereshevskii ("S"), a Russian newspaper reporter in Moscow, who became the famous subject of Alexander R. Luria's classic psychological research study published in 1968.

You might think somebody with such an exceptional memory would be destined for greatness. Unfortunately, the constant build-up of images in "S's" mind ultimately handicapped the man who spent a great deal of time and energy unsuccessfully formulating techniques to forget things and reduce the stress on his mind. Though "S" held many different jobs trying to find his niche, he eventually settled on being a professional mnemonist performing memory stunts in a circus act. Perhaps, "S's" greatest contribution to humanity was his remarkable story told in the book, *The Mind of a Mnemonist*, written by the psychologist who spent thirty years of his life observing and working with the man who could not forget.

Memory Workout
Memory Crossword

To complete the crossword puzzle, determine what type of memory is characterized by the clue provided below. Shaded boxes represent a break in the word. Crossword puzzles provide a wonderful way to exercise your memory. Many people who retain sharp memory well into their senior years report they've always done crossword puzzles.

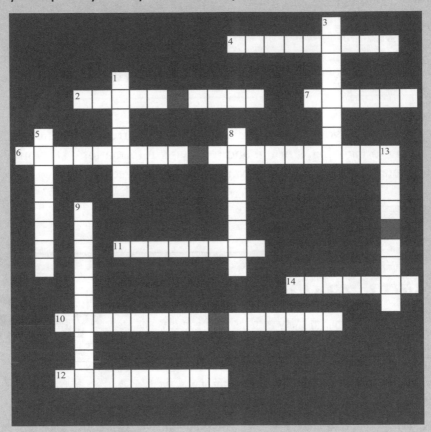

1. Another term for short-term memory

2. Holds information for up to about twenty seconds or longer if rehearsed

3. Stored consciously or voluntarily

4. Retrieves information instantly and instinctually helping to keep us safe

5. Stored unconsciously or involuntarily

6. Lasts less than one second

7. Perceived through the eyes and stored as concrete images

8. Includes academic and professional knowledge

9. Involves skills or learned tasks

10. Best retrieved by rhymes, jingles, acrostics, and verbal associations

11. Driven by location and circumstances

12. Like a moment frozen in time

13. Holds information for up to a lifetime

14. Involves the input of data perceived through the senses

* answer key on page 188 in the Appendix

*C*hapter Recollections

- Why are some kinds of information easier for you to remember than others?

- What are the three types of memory that are represented by the memory-duration model, and how do they differ?

- What is the primary difference between explicit and implicit memory? These memory types are also known by what other names?

- What kind of memory is relied upon most in an academic environment? How does this memory type differ from episodic memory?

- What is the value of reflexive memory? How is the processing, storage, and retrieval of this memory distinct from other memory types?

- What kinds of things do you do everyday that rely on procedural memory?

- Think about your favorite restaurant and consider what sensory memories come to mind.

- The memory system is a complex interaction of what biological elements?

- What considerations are taken into account by the brain in the memory encoding process?

- In what simple ways can understanding the basic memory formation, storage, and retrieval process improve our memory?

- What seven factors contribute to forgetting? Do any of these resonate with your personal experience?

- What six circumstances help us remember? Can you think of others?

- Do you know what your preferred memory modality might be? What are some examples?

- What questions come to your mind regarding the seven basic memory principles introduced in this chapter?

What's Ahead?

Memory Oddities

Chapter 2

Where Are We Today in the Study of Memory?

Imagine for a moment the following scenario: The most prolific thinkers of all time are magically restored to life for a weekend to examine the current state of affairs in the study of memory. The room is pulsating with energy. Everyone's interest is intensely aroused—from Plato and Aristotle to Freud and Einstein. The luminaries are addressed by a Nobel-Prize winning scientist who announces that, after thousands of years, the most beguiling aspect of memory—its very nature—has, indeed, been solved; and with empirical evidence, to boot. Once the rustle of excitement stills in the room, the speaker proceeds.

The oldsters look a bit befuddled to hear, however, that memory is *not* a mixture of light and dark or heat and cold as proposed by Parmenides in the sixth century BC; nor is it a process of air distribution in the body as proposed by Diogenes of Apollonia in the fifth century BC. It's not as simple as an imprint on a wax tablet that inevitably wears away over time as Plato advanced in the fourth century BC; nor is it produced by animal spirits as the Greco-Roman physician Claudius Galen suggested in the second century AD. What then is it? At last, the presenter imparts that memory is an electro-chemical signaling process, whereby NEURONS throughout the CORTEX with links to the nervous system communicate with each other via SYNAPSE interaction—a finding she declares, that was impossible to make before the development of PET scans and other sophisticated neuro-imaging devices incorporated in the 1980s and 1990s. The audience erupts, at this point, with a flurry of questions and comments.

Eventually the discussion advances from the physiological mechanisms of everyday memory to the less common, but curious phenomenons and mysteries of memory that remain. The presenter broaches the subject of "transplanted" memory with some trepidation as she explains that some heart transplant patients are experiencing "memories" that don't belong to them and that these "borrowed memories," in some cases, have definite links to the personality of the deceased donor. Perhaps, the Egyptians were onto something, she continues, in estimating that the heart is the seat of the soul. The scholars wear ethereal smiles as they attempt to absorb what they're hearing. They agree to return for another forum in the new millennium to address the growing agenda: transplanted memories, phantom limbs, deja vu, universal consciousness, near-death experiences, tip-of-the-tongue phenomenon, past-life memories, extreme memory, and virtual memory. This chapter, thus, takes us on an exploration of these topics that continue to perplex even the brightest scientists of our day.

*C*an Memories Be Transplanted?

A handful of studies pose the question does memory reside in our cells? And if so, can it be transferred from one living organism to another? This may sound like the stuff of science fiction, but some research findings have suggested that worms, rats, and perhaps, even some human beings may have been the recipients of transplanted memories. It is a curios question worth exploring, even though the evidence is considered highly suspect by many respected scientists.

Thinking is a process of remembering, an awareness of something always known, but forgotten.

—Plato

Case Study
Hearts Remember

In 1988, writer Paul Pearsall found himself in the hospital without a concrete diagnosis but with a vague feeling that his heart was trying to tell him something about his health. Upon his insistence, a CAT scan was conducted. The results showed that a massive tumor had developed in his hip that had already progressed to Stage IV lymphoma—a deadly form of cancer. While waiting in the organ-transplant wing of the hospital for a bone-marrow transplant, Pearsall felt that his heart was speaking more boldly to him than ever before. "It told me that there were people with 'good' hearts all around me, including my wife and son, and that my own heart could find healing power by resonating with theirs. It also told me that despite the grim diagnosis, I did not 'have' cancer. Rather, my cells had lost their memory of how to reproduce in a balanced, harmonious way."

Eventually through combined treatments: radiation, a bone-marrow transplant, and support from the hearts of loved ones, Pearsall says his health was restored. His recovery and the stories of other patients he met along the way inspired him to delve deeper into the notion that our heart communicates with our brain. Organ transplant recipients and their families became the center of his work as they shared astonishing accounts with him. *The Heart's Code* (1999), Pearsall's newest book, is the culmination of his personal experience and interviews with 150 organ donors and their families.

The stories offer fascinating evidence (albeit anecdotal) of what has been coined by some as "cellular memory." Pearsall tells of a little girl who shortly after receiving her new heart was plagued by dreams of being chased by a group of men. After talking with her, police were able to track down the gang who had killed her donor. A fifty-two-year-old man was surprised by his sudden desire to rock out to loud music but it made sense: He learned his heart donor had been a teenager who loved rock-and-roll. A forty-one-year-old man had visions of being surrounded by high-power machinery that would kill him. Only later did he discover that his new heart had belonged to a teenage girl who was killed when her car was struck by a train. One woman developed severe lower-back pains after receiving the heart of a man who was fatally shot in the same place. About 10 percent of organ recipients, Pearsall reports, find themselves experiencing changed sexual appetites, new food cravings and hobbies, different facial expressions, or sudden unrelated health problems following transplant surgery. These interesting cases, of course, do not prove that memory resides in our cells, but they have renewed spirited debates regarding the very nature of the heart and memory. If it's true that the heart "thinks," that cells remember, that the soul is largely a set of cellular memories carried by our heart, and that communication can therefore transcend the boundaries of space and time, then we may soon be admitting what ancient cultures have claimed all along—the heart remembers!

A Worm of Truth

Studies dating back to the mid-1950s purported that memory, stored as molecules in the brain, could be passed from subject to subject. The subjects in psychologist James McConnell's famous work were worms or more specifically, Planaria—a type of flatworm found in freshwater riverbeds. McConnell, affiliated with the University of Michigan at the time, taught his worms to cringe at the sight of light by repeatedly exposing them to a bright light and simultaneous electric shock.

When the planaria could be depended on to cringe expectantly at the sight of light alone, McDonnell diced up the unlucky invertebrates and fed them to their more fortunate (untrained) relatives. Sure enough when the new group of planaria were tested, they were found to cringe at the sight of light suggesting that, in fact, memory transfer had happened. This highly controversial finding sparked a flurry of studies with rats and other animal subjects resulting in contradictory findings. The hoopla eventually faded along with the peace buttons of the times; but isn't it interesting that just as the fashions of the "hippie era" have made a resurgence, so has the question of transplanted memory.

What Does Phantom Limb Phenomenon Tell Us About Memory?

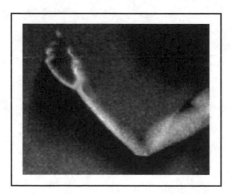

Phantom limb phenomenon may reflect our brain's most current sensory information stored in memory, which in an amputee's case, is likely pain.

University of California at San Diego neuroscientist V.S. Ramachandran describes in his book *Phantoms in the Brain* (1998) one of the most intriguing memory aberrations in current scientific literature—phantom limbs. This phenomenon, in which an amputee or patient with a paralyzed limb feels pain in the compromised area and, in some cases, believes it is still there and functioning, provides a rich laboratory in which to study the role of the unconscious in memory and perception.

Dr. Ramachandran argues that when we perceive information through our senses, a lightening fast process of comparison with previous learning (or memory) occurs to organize and encode the perception. Basically, the theory goes that a non-physically challenged subject will receive sensory signals from a healthy limb, which provides feedback that is current and ongoing. An amputee or paralysis victim, on the other hand, lacking current sensory information, will remember the most current sensory perception they have—likely a (pre-existing) pain memory.

Although, the interplay between vision and imagination and pain and memory are not completely clear yet, Ramachandran believes that what we call perception is really the end result of a dynamic interface between sensory signals and stored information derived from visual images of the past. Ultimately, if our brain does not receive confirming visual stimuli, it is free to simply make up its own reality. A form of "mirror therapy," devised by Ramachandran, helps patients reconnect old pain and perceptions with feedback that is more current, accurate, and productive.

When Deja Vu Occurs, Are You Remembering a Forgotten Past?

The French word deja vu, meaning "already seen," was first used in the late nineteenth century to describe one of the most perplexing phenomena associated with memory—the feeling of having encountered a situation before though having no conscious memory of it. Deja vu happens spontaneously and instantaneously with no warning. It cannot be predicted, anticipated, or encouraged. One moment you're strolling through the park, and the next, you're swept into a feeling of having lived through this exact moment before—perhaps, reencountering some sensory stimuli or feelings from some forgotten dream or previous lifetime?

Deja vu can leave a person feeling baffled or concerned for their mental health, but it is not uncommon, nor does it mean you are "losing your mind." The unexplained feeling of familiarity may, in fact, be the result of a particular electrochemical interaction in your brain. Though psychologists and memory experts have yet to definitively decipher the source of deja vu, we do know that the sensation is likely activated in the brain's bilateral TEMPORAL LOBES.

Neuroscientists have found they can trigger the sensation of deja vu in healthy subjects by administering electrical stimulation to the temporal lobe areas of the brain.

Deja vu has been explained by some as a double awareness, whereby we suddenly become acutely aware of ourselves being aware of our surroundings evoking an instantaneous distortion of new sensations that may feel like a memory.

The deja vu phenomenon has been at the center of spirited debates among psychologists and psychiatrists for many years. Upon noting that the sensation often follows injury to the temporal lobes and is commonly experienced by people with temporal lobe epilepsy, neuroscientists found they could trigger the sensation in healthy subjects through electrical stimulation to this area.

What about, however, the occurrences of deja vu that most of us (presumably healthy subjects) have experienced without electrical stimulation to the brain? There are various theories. Some psychologists believe that they may be the result of a memory fragment or a combination of elements in a present situation that somehow evokes a specific past experience unidentifiable by the conscious mind. Others believe it is a sensory-processing anomaly in which the brain mistakes a fresh impression for a remembered impression complete with meaning, context, and the sense of recognition that accompanies a vivid memory. Still, others attribute the phenomenon to a brief state of hyper-consciousness in which a mild mental dissociation or semi-detachment occurs. Although we can't say for certain what triggers deja vu, we can say with impunity that it reminds us just how complex our memory system is.

Could a Universal Consciousness Impact Your Memory?

Do you ever wonder how it is that you know something you don't ever remember learning? For centuries inquiring minds have attempted to explain the nature of such energy or information transfer. Although, this is another subject that has not been proven empirically, there are those who believe that a Universal Consciousness of sorts informs their personal memory. The phenomenon is known by various terms—collective conscience, collective unconscious, karma, synchronicity, universal energy, morphic fields, M-fields, and universal knowledge. They all, however, refer to the same concept—a memory pattern that is linked through resonance (a form of vibration) to the aura or energy field of another object. For eons religious followers and international scientists—from Russia to China and from ancient Hawaii to Washington DC—have postulated that energy fields shape all living forms of matter. Not until the 1980s, however, when the world discovered bio-magnetics and bio-electricity, did a possible explanation for universal consciousness exist.

Each person is at each moment capable of remembering all that has happened to him [her] and of perceiving everything that is happening everywhere in the universe.

—Aldous Huxley
The Doors of Perception

The morphic field (or M-field), as it is called by biologist Rupert Sheldrake and author of *The Presence of the Past* (1988), "sets up a soundless resonance that—along with genetics—influences and shapes every fiber of every being." The idea, writes Dr. Sheldrake is that "the ease and speed with which you learn a particular task is related to how many times someone—anyone—has done it before you."

The famous Swiss psychologist Carl Jung, who also supported this collective notion of memory wrote, "The collective unconscious contains the whole spiritual heritage of mankind's evolution, born anew in the brain structure of every individual." Jung, whose goal was to assist his clients in realizing the vast potential of their unconscious mind, noted a possibly related phenomenon he called synchronicity—the seeming coincidental occurrence of related events or images in a short time period. In Jungian terms, many of these oddly fortuitous "coincidences" are the result of energy forces engineered on both a personal and collective unconscious level. Every person, tree, rock, and grain of sand on the planet, the theory goes, carries with it in its M-field universal memory. Although all of us can attest to knowing things we don't ever remember learning, the explanations for the phenomenon of universal memory have yet to be supported by empirical or biological evidence.

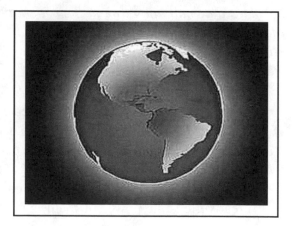

The notion of a collective consciousness has been explained as the existence of a energy field surrounding every person, tree, rock, and grain of sand on the planet that carries with it a pattern of universal memory. This concept, however, has not been proven empirically.

What Do Near-Death Experiences Tell Us About Memory?

NDEers remember their experience even though the body is shut down; and it's not a vague recollection. Rather, it's a superpotent memory that becomes a demarcation line in their identity and life thereafter. Near-death experiences can't be dismissed easily: There are simply too many of them with too many similarities.

Most people have known someone or read an account of a person who believed they were very near death's door, only to be brought back to life with an exceptionally clear account of the experience and the events of their life. In recent years, reports of near-death experiences (NDEs) have become much more common, likely due to resuscitation advances that enable doctors to "bring people back from the dead." A Gallup Poll conducted in the 1980s reported that more than 8 million Americans with remarkably similar accounts had experienced the life-changing effects of a NDE.

One of the common threads reported by NDE experiencers is that your whole life "flashes before you." When this occurs, the brain somehow reduces a lifetime into seconds or minutes. Some people believe that this "life-review" (also known as panoramic memory) lends testimony to the argument that all long-term memories are stored in their entirety in the brain; and that the primal, creative, cosmic power of them is greatly underestimated by our current culture.

The testimonies of near-death survivors reveal eight other common aspects of the experience, as well. Not all of them, however, are usually present in each situation; and only one of them needs to be to constitute an NDE. The general sequence includes: a sense of being dead, peace and painlessness, a sense of being out of body, passing through a tunnel, meeting beings of light, a life review, a rise into the heavens, and a reluctance to return. The life-review aspect of the experience, claim many NDE survivors, is presented in the third-person perspective almost as if you're watching a movie. The person not only sees every significant action they've taken in life, but the effects of those actions on others, as well. If the accounts of near-death experiencers are accurate, there may be some truth to the final judgement scenario prophesied by many major religions. It may be, however, that rather than being judged by a "superior being," we are destined to judge ourselves in the context of a total perspective reserved for death or near-death.

Years of investigation into the NDE phenomenon have provided us with hundreds of thousands of testimonies from people around the globe, from all walks of life and belief systems and in all age brackets. However numerous these reports are, scientists point out that this does not constitute empirical evidence. Raymond Moody, psychiatrist and author of the landmark book *Reflections on Life After Life* (1977), and more recently, *Coming Back: a Psychiatrist Explores Past-Life Journeys* (1991), nonetheless believes that the phenomenon provides interesting revelations about memory. NDEers remember their experience even though the body is shut down; and it's not a vague recollection. It's a superpotent memory that becomes a demarcation line in their identity and life thereafter. NDE is so powerful an experience that oftentimes the survivor's identity is split into "before" and "after" the experience. Near-death experiences can't easily be dismissed: There are just too many accounts of them containing too many similarities. Those who are closest to the study of this incredible phenomenon argue that memory is stored in an energy field that is part of a universal field of consciousness that serves as a permanent memory register. Today's neurologists, however, are still seeking scientific evidence to support the vast quantity of anecdotal reports.

How Does a Memory Get Stuck on the Tip of Your Tongue?

The terribly frustrating experience of knowing something, but being unable to recall it in the moment is universal; and chances are it's happened to you more than once. Known as tip-of-the-tongue phenomenon, this form of mental block or temporary memory lapse has been examined by cognitive psychologists since the mid-1960s. Although we have yet to fully explain it, the prevailing theory suggests that a word can get stuck in our mind when the necessary retrieval cue is absent. This would explain why, in most cases, the missing word is usually recovered within a few minutes; and why when the block is not cleared right away, it is most often resolved effortlessly later when a different pathway is accessed or the right association is made.

Stress is often the culprit in such forgetting episodes. Most of us have probably experienced the frustration of knowing you know the answer to a test question, but time is running out and you must move on. If the memory is not recovered, however, it may be that a closely related or similarly sounding word has become lodged in the mind and, in a sense, cancels out the right word. In this case, the common advice is to change your current context and try again later. Reconstructing a sequence of events in your mind, visualizing the circumstances or related concepts, or running through the alphabet while sounding out possible associations may also help trigger the missing cue.

Another explanation for tip-of-the-tongue phenomenon is that it is merely a memory-organization problem. Consider, for example, how difficult it might be to retrieve a specific piece of information from a book that has been poorly indexed and that lacks a table of contents. It is likely that our memory operates by a similar system. We are certain we know something, but we can't find it. When asked to recall, for example, the countries that border Switzerland, you might be unsuccessful when attempting to do so blindly; however, when provided with a list of possible answers you recognize the correct ones immediately. Thus, we see that a particular item may be poorly catalogued in our mental library; and unless we locate the appropriate cue or clue, it remains irretrievable. In contrast, when we are provided with a starting place or a narrowed field of choices, the answer becomes recognizable.

Remembering a word can depend on its sound, image, or meaning. Thus, encoding a word by linking it to a similar sound, visual, and/or definition can be a powerful strategy for reducing the frequency of tip-of-the-tongue experiences. For example, after a particularly frustrating tip-of-the-tongue jam I experienced recently with the word "compound" (as in, one problem compounds another), I linked in my mind the visual image of a mad scientist mixing or "compounding" two substances and the sound of the word "composition" meaning a unity of parts to prompt my memory in the future. Since enacting this cue, "compound" has ceased to confound me.

Reduce your tip-of-the-tongue occurrences by becoming more aware of the times when you might be:

- **Distracted or interrupted**
- **Anxious, stressed, or rushing**
- **Elated or depressed**
- **Fatigued or sick**

- Under the influence of alcohol or drugs
- Lacking some information necessary for understanding
- In a familiar setting; on autopilot
- Constrained by time; therefore, unable to process or organize the information

When these circumstances are present, try:

- Taking a mental snapshot of the thing you want to remember
- Visualizing the information in pictures or images related to each other and applying a sound-alike mnemonic (i.e., the name Jack Lander becomes a jack-o'-lantern)
- Slowing down and consciously relaxing
- Tuning into your senses; pay closer attention and shut out distractions
- Recognizing that it's not a good time to try and remember new information

Figure 2.1

Body Memories

Some evidence suggests that memories may be stored in the entire body, not just the brain. The transport system for such, scientists believe, may be PEPTIDE MOLECULES which circulate throughout the body via the bloodstream. In addition, memory may reside within body tissue (cellular memory), as evidenced by the accounts of organ (especially heart) transplant patients who claim that along with the organ they received from their donor came memories, likes, dislikes, and personality changes that did not previously belong to them. This phenomenon sparks the question, what are memories really made of?

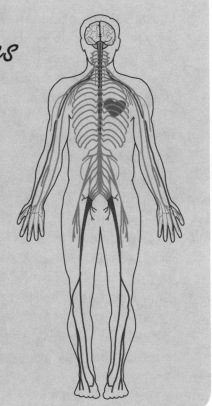

Memory Workout
Implicit Memory Retrieval Quiz

The brain encodes some experiences and information indelibly without conscious effort, while other types of information that are not survival-oriented must be repeated, encoded, and rehearsed for long-term storage. The simple memory questions that follow illustrate how knowledge that is stored in unconscious (implicit) memory may be problematic to retrieve on demand; nevertheless, they are stored somewhere. Numerous studies conducted with subjects who have amnesia have supported the hypothesis that although explicit memory may be completely compromised, the subject's implicit memory can remain intact. We all have a storehouse of unconscious memories that are available, although not necessarily easily accessible.

Just how difficult is it to retrieve knowledge even if we encounter it daily over many years? Take a few minutes to answer the following questions and find out.

1. **On a traffic signal light, which color is at the top—red or green?**

2. **Try to visualize a pushbutton telephone. Sketch the configuration of all the numbers, plus the star and pound sign.**

3. **On the spine of a book, is the title right side up or upside down when the book is laid face up? (Hint: American and British books have different conventions.)**

4. **What are the highest and lowest numbers on your oven dial; how about on your car speedometer?**

5. **On a U.S. dollar bill, which direction does George Washington face?**

6. **Of all the former statesmen pictured on U.S. bills between $1 and $100, two are non-presidents. Can you name them?**

7. **On a penny, which direction does Abraham Lincoln face?**

8. **We all know how many stars there are on the U.S. flag, but how many rows are they arranged into? How many stars are in each row?**

* Answer key on page 188 in the appendix.

Are Past-Life Memories Real?

Reincarnation is the belief that the soul survives and returns to Earth in another form after the death of the physical body. The belief in reincarnation and past-life memories dates back to at least the third century BC when the Greek philosopher, Plato, espoused that the human spirit goes through nine cycles of rebirth

Karma is memory.

—Edgar Cayce

until eventually reaching the ninth and highest level, at which time we are freed from our earthly journey. The Egyptians, too, believed in rebirth; and that the cycle of our spirit continues for three thousand years. However, in 325 AD Emperor Constantine officially declared the belief in reincarnation a Christian heresy punishable by death; and as a result, the concept kept alive only in secret, has long been held suspect. Although a great deal of anecdotal evidence suggests that some people may, in fact, retain memory from past lives, many scientists debunk the claims for lack of scientific evidence.

In spite of the skepticism, the claims endure. As Eastern religions, with a fundamental belief in reincarnation, have spread to the West, so has a renewed interest in reincarnation in this century. Thomas Edison and Henry Ford were both known believers in reincarnation, as are many famous personalities living today—among them Shirley MacLaine and Sylvester Stallone. Joan Grant, a famous British author and powerful psychic who coined the term "far" memories, revealed in her book *Far Memory* (1956) that she was sharing her own past-life memories in her previous seven best-selling historical novels. Quite surprisingly, archaeologists were able to validate many of her book's previously undocumented background details as historical fact.

Other accounts of reincarnation were described by Dr. Ian Stevenson who conducted a series of scientific investigations into the phenomenon between 1946 and 1966. One of the most provocative cases, reported in his book *Twenty Cases Suggestive of Reincarnation* (1974), involved Shanti Devi, born in Delhi, India in 1926. At the age of seven, Shanti announced to her parents that she had lived ten years previously in the distant town of Muttra as a woman named Ludgi. Through a series of chance and then, planned events, the girl identified all of her relatives still living from her previous life. First she met a cousin, then her husband and two of their three children (the third she died giving birth to)—all with accurate details and knowledge that could not be explained otherwise. She identified details about the city of Muttra, which she had not visited in her present lifetime. As she walked the streets blindfolded, the girl pointed out directions and buildings and spoke in a local dialect to which she had not been presently exposed to. Stories of a similar nature have been recounted the world over. Some people believe past-life learning is the most viable explanation for child prodigies like Wolfgang Amadeus Mozart who began composing music at age four and made his first professional tour through Europe as a pianist when he was six.

Some people believe that past-life learning is the most viable explanation for child prodigies like Wolfgang Amadeus Mozart who began composing at age four.

Even so, some authorities insist that the past-life recaller may merely be confusing a vivid hallucination with a past-life memory. Others believe the memories may be "manufactured" in therapy sessions utilizing hypnotic trance techniques for "memory recovery." Still others suggest that the subjects may be picking up information from "universal memory" or universal consciousness, a subject reviewed previously in this chapter. The difficulty in proving the phenomenon of past-life memory is obvious. How does one go about constructing a reliable proof for the memory of something that may have happened in a different millennium? This is not a new question; nor is it likely to be answered real soon. The subject, however, remains fascinating and deeply-rooted in human consciousness.

*H*ow Might We Explain the Existence of Extreme Memory?

Many psychologists downplay the "magical" properties associated with exceptional memory abilities, known by scientists as hypermnesia; and emphasize that it is, rather, normal memory developed to an extreme. Performance-oriented mnemonists certainly demonstrate the incredible potential of our memory, but some suspect their abilities are sensationalized for entertainment value. What is commonly known as photographic memory is more accurately eidetic imagery—the ability to remember in sharp detail an image as if it were a snapshot captured in the mind. The term *eidetic*, which means identical, may imply infallible; however, nobody's memory is infallible. Since an image in the mind is only as good as the subject's initial perception of it, all memory has the potential to be faulty. Distortions and omissions do occur; and since what is stored in short-term memory does not, by default, make it to long-term memory, even memory geniuses can forget.

Nevertheless, some people do demonstrate exceptional memory abilities, as evidenced by accounts of the "memory geniuses" profiled in Chapter 5. People with extreme memory abilities usually have magnified sensory perception in one or more of their senses. For example, eidetic imagery implies acute visual perception. Other memory geniuses may have exceptional hearing, smell, taste, or a combination of sensory attributes. It is estimated that one in 500,000 people are born with a condition called SYNESTHESIA, whereby the individual's sensory perceptions are involuntarily crosslinked. As such, they associate words, sounds, and objects with colors, tastes, and shapes often resulting in extreme-memory ability, but also in difficulties related to other areas of their life (see Case Study: The Man Who Could Not Forget in Chapter 1).

Except in rare cases, people who exhibit extreme memory are most likely applying learned MNEMONIC techniques (consciously or unconsciously) exceptionally well. Although approximately 5 to 10 percent of children exhibit exceptional memory in early childhood, most do not retain it into adulthood. This fact supports the theory that we all have vast unused memory potential ripe for the plucking. It has been argued that many children are born with an innate photographic memory ability that we train away by emphasizing too much logic and language at the expense of imagination and creativity.

Most cases of exceptional memory are reflective of a particular memory-type strength; for example, the ability may be specifically in remembering names and faces, a long series of numbers, complex patterns or images, volumes of poetry, or vastly intricate musical scores. If an exceptional memory is the result of the utilization of memory principles, does this mean that any of us can develop a super-memory? Conceivably, yes! But this is a little bit like asking if anyone can become a world-class high jumper? Potentially, we can excel to this degree; however, achieving world-class mastery of anything requires exceptional commitment, concentration, practice, and support.

Except in rare cases, people who exhibit extreme memory are most likely applying learned mnemonic techniques (consciously or unconsciously) exceptionally well.

This, however, is the extreme; but on average most people can improve their memory a great deal. After reading this book and applying a few simple memory strategies, you can expect noticeable improvement in your memory, even with minimal effort. Of course, the more you work at it, the more dramatic the results will be.

*V*irtual Memory:
What Does the Future Hold?

Scientific inquiry has extended far beyond what memory is: For decades scientists have been considering the possibilities of what memory could be. Laboratories around the world buzz with progress in the areas of artificial intelligence (AI), therapeutic mind machines, memory scanning and mapping equipment, memory manipulation methods, and memory prompting through electrical stimulation. If all this sounds like a sci-fi novel to you, then the fiction of yesteryear may be closer to today's reality than you realized. Let's take a glance at this fascinating world of virtual memory as it is evolving today.

Even if one were to figure conservatively that we keep very little in active memory—say one-tenth of 1 percent of whatever we learn in life—it would still mean that our active memories hold several billion times more information than a large research computer.

—Morton Hunt
The Universe Within

■ *Artificial Intelligence*

Among the innovations we've come to expect from a forward-looking company like Xerox is the development of a second-generation memory "prostheses" device dubbed "Vepys." Producing a minute-by-minute video recording of a person's movements, Vepys developed at the EuroParc laboratory in Cambridge, England, is the closest thing to artificial memory we have to date. Its effectiveness, however, is still only as good as the information it records, which is collected by infrared recognition of a person wearing a specially-tagged identification badge. Much like the automated toll-collection systems now in effect on impacted freeways in large urban centers, the infrared captures information as the target passes. As memory-preservation technology like camcorders and cameras linked to computer programs continues to improve, so will AI technology. A micro-computer system, for example, has been fitted to Vepys which allows it to cross-reference the information it gathers in a seemingly logical fashion. The future of artificial memory, as evidenced by the interest in robot technology, is bright; however, the most powerful microchip in the world has yet to come close to the highly analytical and ultra-complex nature of the human mind and memory system.

■ *Therapeutic Mind Machines*

Many variations of mind tools or cognitive-enhancement machines have evolved over the past few decades. From *sensory-reduction* devices like flotation tanks to *sensory-enhancement* devices like music and light-modulation domes and goggles, thousands of people have reported their benefits. The claim of heightened mental powers following a session may hold true relative to the device's ability to alter the user's brain chemistry or brainwave activity, induce a highly focused state of relaxation and suggestibility, or increase mental imagery and visualization control. Inducing a "peak-performance state" (like hypnotherapy), may stimulate a level of receptivity not normally reached in day-to-day living. Some practitioners and researchers who have used these devices with clients report profound effects, including increased memory, IQ, creativity, and sexual pleasure; and reduced pain and depression; as well as and breakthroughs in drug-addiction treatment (Hutchison 1994). Users claim their experiences with mind machines have induced great pleasure at the very least; and on the other end of the continuum, have been "life changing."

■ *Memory Scanning, Mapping, and Prompting*

The same technology that has allowed scientists to look inside the brain without surgery, is also helping scientists map the areas of the brain where various memories and task-related functions may be encoded and stored. With the advent of neural-imaging devices, it is not farfetched to think that in the not-so-distant future, a "forgotten" memory might be located, stimulated, and recovered electronically.

Wilder Penfield, a Canadian neurosurgeon studying epilepsy in the 1930s demonstrated—even to his own surprise—that when particular brain cells were stimulated with a minute electric current, some patients would experience a very vivid sensory "flashback" of a moment from their past. These now famous studies have been the subject of controversy; but despite what they do or don't tell us about the nature of memory, they offer a glimpse into a possible future, whereby memory might be prompted at will through precise stimulation.

■ *Memory Control*

Rumors that the CIA was experimenting with memory manipulation on human subjects surfaced in the era of the cold-war. It wasn't until 1976, however, that the CIA would come under investigation for this unthinkable atrocity. Eventually ten Canadian victims would be compensated a million dollars each for losing large chunks of their memory as a result of the CIAs effort (funded through a Canadian front known as the Society for the Investigation of Human Ecology) to create the perfect spy. Ex-CIA agents provided evidence that projects secretly coded MK-ULTRA were set up to artificially seed multiple personalities, repattern personality, and wipe out memory. Credible sources reported that the extent of the CIAs research went far beyond the lab setting. Victims were unwittingly used as spies after being programmed to carry out dangerous foreign missions of which they would retain no memory. Worse yet, the subject's programming called for them to commit suicide when they were no longer useful to the CIA—the ultimate weapon, perhaps, in the control of the human mind (Ostrander and Schroeder 1991).

While world-renowned scholars introduced at the beginning of this chapter concern themselves with issues such as human-knowledge transfer via cell implants and gene splicing, and the implantation of human memory prosthetic devices downloaded from the ultimate memory server, we shall save these topics for the next book. Meanwhile, let's get down to some nitty-gritty memory-enhancement techniques that will improve your memory functioning right away!

Memory Booster
The Write Touch

Most people have had the experience of remembering a dream just after waking up and then promptly forgetting it. If you want to remember something accurately, the experts recommend that you write it down in detail immediately afterward. Bank tellers are often instructed to use this strategy in the event of a robbery. To reduce the possibility of distortion, the experience ought to be recorded before talking with anyone else or proceeding with other activities (more on memory distortion in Chapter 8).

When you go to bed tonight, place your memory journal by your bed with a pen or pencil beside it. As soon as you wake up, take a few minutes to record what you were dreaming about. Supply as much detail as possible. Don't ignore anything you can remember, even though it may seem insignificant. Author Patricia Garfield, Ph.D. in her book *Creative Dreaming* (1975) says that "if you have trouble remembering your dreams, don't worry. It is within anyone's power to master dream recall." The more you remember and study them, the more you'll get out of them.

Chapter Recollections

- What is meant by "transplanted memories"?

- What theory might explain the phenomenon of phantom limbs?

- Have you ever experienced deja vu? Which explanation for it do you feel is most plausible?

- In what way is "synchronicity" comparable to "universal consciousness"?

- What do many near-death recollections have in common? What might these common experiences tell us about the nature of memory?

- What are some of the factors that may contribute to a tip-of-the-tongue occurrence?

- What evidence is there to support the claim that some people can remember past lives? Do you feel the evidence sufficiently explains the phenomenon?

- What are some of the misconceptions about people who exhibit extreme-memory powers?

- How might our future be impacted by the reality of virtual memory?

What's Ahead?

Your Personal Memory Toolbox

How Much Can I Expect to Improve My Memory?

When we talk about improving memory, we aren't talking about something as concrete or measurable as say, cardiovascular fitness. Improving recall is rather like improving your golf game—a mass of dynamics are involved. As such, there is no single secret to developing a great memory. Since there are as many different types of memory as there are golf clubs, learning a host of memory techniques is recommended. The principles presented in this chapter provide the foundation for the effective use of a system of memory aids known collectively as MNEMONICS. However, as with perfecting your tee shot, putt, and drive, applying the principles and practicing good technique is what guarantees your success. Applying memory principles is simple and fun. When utilized, even minimally, you'll begin tapping into your fullest memory potential.

The capacity of human memory is difficult to measure under ordinary circumstances. However, recent brain research has confirmed what experts have always claimed: Our brain is capable beyond our wildest expectations. In fact, some scientists estimate that the average brain can hold as many as one quadrillion bits (that's 1 followed by 15 zeroes) of information in long-term memory.

Our brains, however, are designed to retain meaningful versus random bits of information. Thus, remembering an arbitrary social security number or an esoteric concept requires a more complex strategy than remembering Saturday's tee time or massage appointment—presumably something you covet. The average person can only memorize three to five bits or chunks of random information at a time, but each of these can have an additional three to five chunks within it—somewhat like the Russian doll sets where each doll is contained within a larger one. So even though a social security number, for instance, is nine numbers (chunks) long, when reduced to three smaller subsets, it can be remembered quite easily. This strategy, called CHUNKING, demonstrates how the brain can be trained to work more efficiently—to process and recall greater quantities of data. Most of the principles (or tools) outlined in this chapter incorporate ways to purposefully encode (or cue) information as a type of retrieval "insurance."

■ *The Role of Mnemonics*

Essentially, mnemonics (pronounced neh-mon-iks) are memory tools. The origin of the word dates back a millennium or more. The ancient Greeks so revered the power of memory that a goddess named Mnemosyne—meaning "mindful"—was exalted on the same scale of virtues as love and beauty. A host of memory strategies were devised by the Greek and Roman statesmen of the day to help them remember vast amounts of information by which to impress their audiences during senatorial speeches and debates. In present times, the word refers to memory techniques in general. Now that we recognize memory to be a process involving three elements—encoding, maintenance, and retrieval—we have refined and added to the mnemonic techniques once used by the ancient orators.

Remember...

to form a sharp memory of something:

- **The original information must be encoded accurately;**

- **Maintained or strengthened over time; and**

- **Triggered by an association or cue.**

Can Information Be Retrieved Even if It Was Poorly Encoded?

Maybe, but it's not likely that the memory will be accurate. It is more likely that you will *recognize* the information when presented to you, for example, in a multiple-choice format, rather than *recall* it independently as would be required of an essay question. If the information, on the other hand, was poorly encoded, poorly maintained, and a strategic memory technique was not incorporated, there's no hope for data recovery. But each of these three processes gives you a separate chance to increase your odds for success. In fact, every system, tool, memory course, strategy, class, idea, or insight that improves your ability to remember has to do with some or all of these three critical memory stages.

What Strategies Will Help Me Encode Important Information?

Tool # 1: Positive Attitude/Belief

It is of utmost importance that, first, you truly believe you can learn and remember anything you wish. Under these circumstances your body relaxes and directs its full energy to the task at hand. Positive attitude works on multiple levels: It virtually alters the chemistry of your brain. A positive attitude fosters the production of DOPAMINE, a feel-good NEUROTRANSMITTER. Like a pump recycling water through a fountain, optimism promotes dopamine and dopamine, thus, propels optimism. Secondly, positive attitude helps manufacture more quantities of NORADRENALINE, another neurotransmitter, which provides you with the physical energy to act on your motivations. Thirdly, constructive thinking activates the FRONTAL LOBES which are most responsible for long-term planning and judgment. In short, being positive does more than create the "Pollyanna Effect," it actually mobilizes your brain for learning.

Tool #2: Precise Observation

Most of the information our brain is exposed to is nonconscious. Dr. Emanual Donchin, from the University of Illinois Champagne-Urbana, suggests that more than 99 percent of the information we process is nonconscious. To avoid being bombarded by countless floods of sensory trivia, the human brain has learned to attend consciously only to information that is deemed important. In the extreme, as when something threatens our survival, we pay attention. While we all perceive millions of bits of random information per minute, the information that we definitely want to remember must be cued consciously into our memory system. Here's where motivation comes into play. To ensure the incoming data is encoded correctly, your attention and focus must be purposefully engaged. Whether your interest is genuine or not, the extra initiative of focusing your attention can be enough to store and retrieve a memory.

The more you observe, listen, and think about something, the deeper the memory trace will be. Notice if there are any smells present. If so make a mental note of them. Listen for anything unusual—changes in background noise or variations in volume. Write down information that is especially meaningful or important; draw pictures, icons, or figures to illustrate a point; and check out your perception to confirm if it is accurate. Close your eyes and visualize what you're hearing. Mentally review the message and rephrase it in your own words. The more you involve your senses, the stronger the initial memory encoding will be.

When the big picture is perceived first, the details make more sense. In teaching somebody to play golf, for example, keeping score would give them a more contextualized understanding of "par."

Tool #3: Consider Context

Another critical element for encoding a memory is to consider context. Context implies the larger pattern—the meaning, the circumstances, the reason behind the input. When we attend to the big picture first, all the details make more sense. This is the principle that underlies the "What's Ahead?" sections at the beginning of each chapter in this book. We are more likely to understand and remember information when we can see how it fits together. Think about a jigsaw puzzle, for example. A common strategy is to identify the general vicinity of a piece by comparing it to the picture on the box. In other words, the whole provides the necessary context for understanding the parts. Think about learning a new sport. I may not remember, for example, what the terms "par" or "bogie" in golf mean until I've personally played the game and kept score. Likewise, four hundred yards becomes explicitly more meaningful to me upon my repeated attempts to drive the ball that distance.

Tool #4: The BEM Principle

The acronym B.E.M. stands for beginning, end, and middle. When information is presented to you, it is most likely remembered in this sequence. In other words, what is most memorable is what was presented at the beginning; then what was presented at the end; and lastly what was presented in the middle. Why does this happen? Researchers speculate that an attentional bias exists at the beginning and end. The novelty factor inherent in beginnings and the emotional release of endings foster chemical changes in our brain. These changes in our chemistry "tag" the learning and make it more memorable. Thus, if you want to remember information cited in the middle of a presentation, you'll want to apply a memory strategy and pay extra attention to it to ensure that it gets strongly encoded.

Tool #5: Get Active

The concept of active learning is best communicated in the form of an exercise. Consider, therefore, the following two lists—one of numbers and one of letters. Take a few seconds to memorize each list:

14921776181219001917 19631970

NASANBCTVLIPCIAACLU

If this seems difficult, don't worry. It is! In fact, most people have a hard time remembering abstract data, unless they apply a mnemonic strategy—which we're about to do. This time, look again at the numbers and letters, only break them up into groups of three or four and make them meaningful in some way to you. This can be accomplished by connecting the smaller chunks of data to each other with visual images or associations. For example, I associate the first four digits—1492—with a famous date in history (which, of course, is when "Columbus sailed the ocean blue"); then I link it to the next meaningful number sequence with another related image (in this case the signing of the Declaration of Independence). Though we've provided here two fairly obvious examples for the sake of clarity, any sequence of letters or numbers can be remembered using this associative memory technique. Now you do the rest.

What you just did was actually experience through "active learning," the concept of active learning. When a person manipulates information, or experiments with it, or is asked to solve a problem related to it, the data gets encoded along multiple memory pathways—visual, auditory, kinesthetic, etc.—increasing the chance for retrieval.

Manipulating new information creates more associations in your brain and strengthens the ones you have. Here are some tried and true strategies for building memory muscle:

- **Talk about the new learning.**
- **Read about the new learning.**
- **See a movie related to it.**
- **Translate information into symbols— concrete or abstract.**
- **Make a crossword puzzle that utilizes new terms and concepts.**
- **Write a story about the subject.**
- **Draw something related to it.**
- **Discuss new learning in small groups.**
- **Depict new learning through a mind-map.**
- **Make up related rhymes and jingles (i.e., "i before e, except after c, or when sounding like a as in neighbor and weigh.").**
- **Associate physical movements with the new learning (i.e., actors rely on accompanying movements to memorize their lines).**

Tool #6: Chunk It

As demonstrated in the preceding active learning example, complex subjects or long strings of information units are more easily understood and remembered when the data is chunked into more manageable segments. Phone numbers, credit cards, and social security numbers, for example, are always chunked into groups of two, three, or four numbers for ease in recall. The conscious brain can only process about five bits of information at one time, but this amount varies depending on the learner's age and prior learning. Generally, infants ages one to three can only remember one piece of information at a time; children three to seven can recall up to two chunks (or steps in instructions); kids ages seven to sixteen can retain up to three chunks; and those older than sixteen can usually manage four or more chunks.

Whatever your age, manipulating abstract data into manageable groupings improves recall. Here's the same two lists previously used in the active learning exercise, only now we've chunked them for you. Of course, there's no correct or incorrect chunking sequences; the only thing that matters is that they're meaningful to you. Although we have used overtly simplistic examples for the sake of demonstration, subsequent strategies will teach you how to make associations for information in which obvious cues aren't inherent.

Chunking for Easy Recall:

The active learning example used on page 47 is now chunked below to create groupings that make the memory encoding process more efficient.

1492 • 1776 • 1812 • 1900 • 1917 • 1963 • 1970

NASA • NBC TV • LIP • CIA • ACLU

Tool #7: Engage Emotions

Anytime a person's emotions are engaged, they are more likely to form a deeper imprint of the event. Excitement, humor, celebration, suspense, fear, surprise, or any other strong emotion stimulates the production of ADRENALINE, while also activating the AMYGDALA. If you've had the experience of being the guest of honor, for example, at a surprise party in which you were truly surprised then you'll recognize the impact of emotion on memory. On such occasions, the event is marked by the release of adrenaline and the activation of the brain's emotional center, the amygdala, thereby strengthening encoding and retrieval.

Phobias provide a classic example of how emotions can get embedded in long-term memory. Let's say you're four years old and the neighborhood bully sneaks up from behind you, thrusts a snake into your face, and yells "Aaahhhh!" The chances are pretty good that, in that instant, a permanent imprint of the incident is formed. Why? Because intense fear triggers a rush of adrenaline—the survival response that prepares the body for fight or flight; thus, biochemically marking the event. as important. A snake or similar stimulus experienced subsequently will likely then trigger the same automatic response for the rest of your life—unconsciously, if not consciously. This kind of powerful encoding can be reframed (in therapy) if it results in an annoying phobia. Due to the deeply rooted nature of phobias, the support of a qualified therapist is usually recommended, however.

Tool #8: Seek Feedback

"Did you see that?!!!" Whenever we see something unusual, our first tendency is to either disbelieve it or to check it out with another person. This is a smart strategy. You want to make sure that what you *think* you saw or heard is what you *truly* saw or heard. Seeking feedback is a natural and essential learning tool that helps us minimize false impressions before inaccurate memories are formed. The process of feedback helps strengthen our perception and, therefore, increases our likeliness of remembering the event or stimulus. Feedback comes in many forms. Asking questions is one. Even if the answer is less than adequate, the personal involvement with the information deepens the encoding of it.

How Can I Maintain or Strengthen a Memory Over Time?

Tool #9: Get Enough Sleep

Studies suggest that the more learning you do during the day, the more dreaming you're likely to do (or need to do) at night. The state in which we dream, known as REM (rapid eye movement), may be a time of learning consolidation. The REM sleep period assumes about 25 percent of our entire night's rest; and it is thought to be critical to memory (Hobson 1994). This premise is supported by the fact that the a portion of the CEREBRAL CORTEX, known to be critical in long-term memory processing, has been shown to be very active during the period of REM sleep. Other studies have shown that the brain activity patterns of rats in the REM stage match the brain patterns of daytime learning sessions. Bruce McNaughton, Ph.D. at the University of Arizona who conducted the rat studies, suggests that during sleep time, the HIPPOCAMPUS is rehearsing the learning sent to it by the cortex. This critical "downtime" period, which generally falls during the last one-third of our sleep time (3 to 6 a.m.), may make the difference between a weak or strong memory.

Tool #10: Do Interval Learning

The brain is not designed for non-stop learning. Processing time is necessary to build the inner wiring necessary for best connectivity and recall. That's why the most successful learning is done in intervals—learn, rest, learn, rest. Schedule some downtime following each ten- to fifty-minute learning session, depending on the complexity of the material and the age of the learner. This time-tested rule for strengthening memory is of critical importance.

Tool #11: Make It Important

Also significant in the maintenance of a memory is the level of importance the individual assigns the information. A good example of this principle is the student who inevitably forgets their homework, but has memorized each player's batting average on their favorite baseball team. Consider the number of television and radio commercials we are bombarded with daily. How many of the phone numbers announced over the air do you remember? Likely none of them—that is, unless, you're looking for the particular item being advertised.

The student who always forgets their homework may be the same kid that's memorized every player's batting average on their favorite baseball team.

Then you'll make a point to remember it. Think about the last time you were introduced to somebody that you really liked. Did you have to ask them their name more than once? The more important the information is to you, the more likely you will remember it.

Tool #12: Use It

Practice has always been the sage advice of good teachers and coaches, and for good reason. Repetition strengthens memory. As the brain absorbs new information, a connection is made between cells. This connection is strengthened each time it is used. New learning should be reinforced with a review ten minutes after the original learning, then again after forty-eight hours, and again after seven days. This spaced repetition ensures a strong connection. The more ways you use or manipulate the new material, the better. For example, immediately after meeting a new person, use their name: "It was a pleasure to meet you Ms. Sulkowsky. Do you have a business card? Hmmmm....Oh, I see, your name ends with an s-k-y. What's the origin of that spelling?" Looking at photographs is another way to strengthen a memory. Surely some of our high school memories would fade faster than a tropical rain-shower were it not for recalling the faces, names, and shared (mis)adventures through the browning pages and humorous inscriptions in old yearbooks.

Tool #13: Put It In Hard Storage

Some people are mistakenly under the impression that the brain is the body's only memory storage/retrieval center. In reality, all of us depend on alternate memory storage devices all the time. Such things as post-it notes, lists, computers, files, friends, strategically placed objects, and calendars all become part of our memory's supporting cast. Each of these examples serves the same purpose: It provides a "hard copy" that aids memory retrieval. Depending on such external memory devices is not an admission of a failing mind; it's merely smart thinking. Spreading out the responsibility for remembering all of the important elements of our busy lives is a strategic way to strengthen your memory system. A task as simple as merely writing down the information you want to remember can strengthen your memory.

Tool #14: Form Habits

Most of us have dozens, maybe even hundreds, of habits that help remind us of our responsibilities and duties in life. Of course, most of us develop these habits unconsciously. They may include flipping our desk calendar to the appropriate day of the week, hanging notes in obvious places, leaving things out that we want to remember to take to school or work, etc. The strategy here is to consciously incorporate habits into your life that will ease the burden on your memory. For example, when you enter the house, always put your car keys

External memory aids such as Post-It notes, lists, files, friends, strategic objects, and calendars, are all part of our memory's supporting cast.

in the same place, preferably in close proximity to the door. Once you've become aware of your habits, you can capitalize on them by linking information you want to remember to them. For example, you might leave the book you want to remember to take to work by your keys. Thus, at the moment you perform your usual routine, your memory is triggered effortlessly.

I find that it also helps to make a quick visual association linked to a habit. Let's say, for example, I want to remind myself to feed the fish when I get home. I already know I'll be using my keys to open the front door, so I visualize myself unlocking the door when a big bucket of water falls on my head with fish in it. This chilling thought (also ludicrous) provides a rich visual, auditory, and kinesthetic reminder that would be hard to forget, even if I wanted to. Of course, a simpler solution may be to store the fish food in the same cabinet as the placemats, which get used normally every day.

What Mnemonic Tools Will Enhance Memory Retrieval?

Most people find that once they've applied a MNEMONIC technique to remember something retrieval becomes easier. Mnemonics always utilize the principle of association. The following basic mnemonic devices will strengthen your memory retrieval with just a little bit of effort. The key to success, however, is applying the strategies once you've learned them.

■ The Loci Method

Loci (meaning location) is a mnemonic device that works by associating a stable set of places or things in a familiar location with your content markers (things you wish to remember). Let's say, for example, you're giving a speech which contains five key elements. Each part of your talk would be linked to (or hung on) a different "peg" that represents a natural order for you. For the sake of example, let's imagine a typical conference room. The large plant by the podium is the first thing you see when you step on stage, so you choose this cue to remind you of the vibrant welcoming remarks you wish to make. The plaques on the wall are selected to remind you of your next topic—the historical significance of your subject. The next element of your speech—the current state of affairs—is linked to the flag at the back of the room. The exit sign over the door is selected to trigger your closing remarks, etc. In developing the use of this system, we recommend that you consistently use the same pegs in a consistent order. Thus, your front door may be your first peg, your entryway your second, your dining room your third, and so on. Additional loci pegs within these rooms can be assigned as well. This strategy was the memory method of choice for the great orators of antiquity. The visual imagery aspect of it makes it an especially helpful tool for visually dominant learners.

> *Learning how to cue oneself is the true art of memory.*
>
> —Danielle Lapp
> *Don't Forget*

■ The Peg-Word System

This mnemonic strategy works under the same principle as the loci method. In fact, it was derived from it. The only difference is that instead of associating a familiar *location* as your content peg, you use a concrete object. Where the loci system is great for remembering speeches or concepts, the peg-word system is great for remembering numbers. The first step is to learn a set of peg-words. It can be one you make up yourself or a pre-established one like that which we've included on the following page. Some people choose rhyming words because they remember them more easily. For example, they incorporate the pegs from the old song *One-Two Buckle My Shoe*. Thus, two is shoe; four is door; six is sticks; eight is gate; and ten is hen. Others prefer peg-words that have personal significance to them. The list we've included is easy to memorize if you say each word aloud, visualize the scenario, and do the physical motion simultaneously. This approach taps into at least three memory pathways: visual, auditory, and kinesthetic.

Sample Peg-Words

Zero is bills:
Throw your hands to the sky and yell, "zero bills!"

One is sun:
Point to the sky and say, "only one sun!"

Two is legs:
Slap your thigh and say, "my own two legs."

Three is bears:
Pat their heads and say, "The Three Little Bears."

Four is wheels:
Hold an imaginary steering wheel and say, "four wheeling!"

Five is fingers:
Hold up one hand and say, "high five!"

Six is a six-pack:
Take a sip from an imaginary soda can and say, "six-pack please!"

Seven is a week:
Look at an imaginary calendar and say, "a good week!"

Eight is a snowman (shaped like an eight):
Eat some imaginary snow and say, "snow is grEight!"

Nine is Cat:
Pet an imaginary cat and say, "nine lives is a long time!"

Ten is a hen:
Cover your ears with your hands and say "don't be a mother hen."

Review the list until you have it memorized. Add your own additional peg-words as you wish. Once you know ten peg-words, you can combine them to remember any number. For example, the number eleven can be associated with a person reaching both hands up towards the sun; or by combining more images, you can create peg-words up to any number. Most numbers will remind you of logical links. For example, twelve can represent a dozen eggs or the number of months in the year; thirteen, perhaps a black cat or an unlucky number; fourteen, a heart for Valentine's Day; and twenty-six, the letters in the alphabet. If you remember concrete objects better than numbers (like most people), the peg-word system will increase your memory reliability. Once you have committed a peg-word system to memory, you can use another mnemonic technique known as linking to further strengthen the encoding process.

The Keyword Method

This mnemonic method has been used by people for years, particularly for remembering words in a foreign language and abstract concepts. It is another form of association whereby a sound-alike word is verbally and visually associated with an abstract one. For example, the Spanish word for hello, *hola*, might be associated with "oh-lah" as in ooh-la-la, good to see you; and the Spanish word for good bye, *adios*, might be associated with the word "audience" and visually linked to a large audience waving good-bye to you. If you find that a word skips your mind on occasion, apply a keyword mnemonic to it and never forget it again. The word paradox, for example, will forever bring to my mind a pair of ducks. The keyword method is especially helpful for remembering names, as you will see in Chapter 4.

The Linking Method

Linking is the process of connecting or associating one word to another with an action or image. It is often used in conjunction with the peg-word system to remember a string of information units in a particular order. Using the preceding peg-words, for example, the phone number 432-1514, could be cued and linked by visualizing (4) wheels being pushed by (3) bears with (2) stubby little legs through a sunny (1) field. The (3) bears raise their (5) fingers up to the hot sun (1) and let the (4) wheels drop to the ground. Or, perhaps, you prefer to simplify the process by combining numbers into sequences. Thus, the phone number 414-1213 can be remembered as 4 wheels carrying a large valentine to a dozen black cats. You can associate any concrete object to another. For example, to remember your grocery list, link the first item (i.e., flour) to the second item (i.e., tonic water) by visualizing flowers in a vase of water. The key to linking is to use your imagination. The link does not have to be logical or realistic. The only thing that matters is that it jogs *your* memory.

Memory Workout

Making a List in Your Head

Create a grocery list on paper. Now close your eyes and visualize the layout of your local grocery store. Look back at your list as necessary, read each item, then visualize where in the store it is located. Now quickly link one item to the next. Review your shopping trip in your mind—where you'll start in the store, how you'll proceed through the departments, and what you need in each. You will become more confident in relying only on your memory as you practice the techniques. To be safe, take your list with you to confirm you remembered everything before checking out. Eventually the only list you'll need is the one in your head.

Case Study

A Picture's Worth a Thousand Words

One of the earliest studies to examine how visual imagery impacts memory was conducted by the English anthropologist Sir Francis Galton in 1883. Galton, the cousin of Charles Darwin, made some significant contributions of his own to humankind—most notable were the dog whistle, his study of heredity and intelligence which became known as eugenics, modern weather-mapping techniques, and the introduction of finger-print identification. When Galton  became interested in mental imagery, he distributed a questionnaire to one-hundred subjects, asking them to recall in detail their morning breakfast while employing visual imagery as they considered their description.

The results proved interesting; and perhaps predicated the idiom, A picture's worth a thousand words. Galton found that the individuals best able to recall their experience produced rich descriptive narrative imbued with visual imagery. Those who exhibited less memory of the experience produced only vague images; and those who drew a blank were unable to produce any images at all. From this simple but telling trial, Galton conjectured that mental images are important to memory; and that people exhibiting the best memory were able to retrieve abundant images and sensations stored within the mind (Galton 1909; Rupp 1998).

■ Acronyms

Often confused with acrostics, an acronym is a single word made from the first letter of each word in a series. A commonly used acronym is NASA, which abbreviates the name of the National Aeronautics and Space Administration. The names of organizations are frequently shortened to acronyms. Another acronym, which has been taught to many school children, helps us remember the five bodies of water that make up The Great Lakes—HOMES (*H*uron, *O*ntario, *M*ichigan, *E*rie, and *S*uperior). A less commonly known acronym is RADAR, which abbreviates the words *ra*dio *d*etecting *a*nd *r*anging. An acronym may sometimes include a second letter from a word in the series (usually a vowel) to make the abbreviation more readable, as is the case of r*a*dar. An acronym does not necessarily have to make a real word. Use your imagination. If you need to remember to do five things when you get home from work (i.e., *P*ack your suitcase, *S*tart the laundry, return a *C*all, find a *B*aby-sitter, and cancel newspaper *S*ubscription), why not cue your memory with the acronym *PS-CBS*. If you've discovered this technique and are using it already, congratulations. You've probably adopted other memory tools unconsciously, as well.

■ *Acrostics*

An acrostic, like an acronym, also utilizes key letters to make an abstract concept more concrete, and thus, more memorable. However, an acrostic does not always utilize the first letter of a word in the association, nor does the association always result in a one-word abbreviation. The information may correspond, for example, to a line or verse. Roy G. Biv is an acrostic that has helped many people recall the order of the visible spectrum of the rainbow: *r*ed, *o*range, *y*ellow, *g*reen, *b*lue, *i*ndigo, and *v*iolet. Other examples include the rhyme "*E*very *g*ood *b*oy *d*oes *f*ine" to remember the notes EGBDF on the lines in the treble clef; and "*M*y *v*ery *e*ducated *m*other *j*ust *s*liced *u*p *n*ine *p*ickles" to remember the order of the planets in our solar system. On a real practical note, I'm remembering my last-minute Thanksgiving grocery list (yams, allspice, butter, milk, flowers, almonds, bread, and dish detergent) with the acrostic *Y*ams *A*nd *B*utter *M*ake *F*or *A* *B*etter *D*inner. I'm hoping it's true; but at least, I know I won't forget anything at the grocery store.

■ *Rhymes and Jingles*

Rhymes and jingles have probably helped you remember information ever since you learned the ABCs to the tune of *Twinkle Twinkle Little Star*. Most, if not all, of the pre-school television learning programs rely heavily on rhymes and jingles to teach children about everything from brushing their teeth to buckling their seatbelts. And long before these wonderful TV learning shows were created, Dr. Seuss and Mother Goose modeled the value of rhymes for remembering through books and storytelling. Material that is inherently easy to forget is especially aided by the magical quality of information set to a tune, rhyming verse, or jingle. For example, who in this country doesn't know what happened in fourteen hundred and ninety-two? And, for a spelling review, when does i come before e? How do you remember which way to move the clock for daylight-savings time? And for practical purposes, how many days does September have? How about April, June, and November?

■ *Mnemonics for Family Fun*

Activities incorporating mnemonics provide an opportunity for a great deal of fun and creativity with children—from road-trip games to dinner time antics. Growing up, for example, in my family, we learned the basic rules of the household from a collection of rhymes that my parents put together called *Rhyming Rules for Children*. This handy rhyming picture book reminded us in a joyful way that "when you're sick, you get your pick; when you're tall enough to touch your toes, you're big enough to pick up your clothes; we share our toys with girls and boys; and take what you're served, eat what you wish, and leave the rest upon your dish." These simple jingles (and many more) are ingrained, to this day, in our family culture—and now the subsequent generation.

Mnemonic techniques of all kinds provide an opportunity for a great deal of fun and creativity with children—from travel games on road trips and everyday learning to lifelong memories.

Another example of instilling memory awareness in children comes to mind upon seeing a photograph of The Grand Canyon. Although the experience occurred thirty-plus years ago, my memory of it is visceral—as my family peered over the edge of one of the world's greatest natural wonders I can almost hear my father making the comment he reserved for the most awe-inspiring moments, "Now, let this sink into your memory cells, kids." And, it did! In like fashion the phrase, "Quartzite, flat tire, beautiful moon," instantly evokes the vivid recollection of our last stretch home after a 6-week cross-country trip. We had just repaired a blow-out in the sweltering Arizona desert and were collectively praying for a hotel to appear out of nowhere. The possibility of another flat tire evoked images of us stranded on a lonely blazing hot stretch of highway lit only by the full moon. We thankfully survived the tense moment, the remaining tires held out, and we eventually welcomed the sight of a dusty fleabag motel with open arms. Ultimately, the memory outlived the danger in a silly little jingle we spontaneously created to mark the moment. The next time your kids ask, "Are we there yet?" think about playing a memory game. Engaging your children's memory is simple, enjoyable, and rewarding entertainment.

Memory Booster
Journal Activity

Describe in your journal how you are currently using some of the principles outlined in this chapter. What techniques might you use to help you encode a memory? How do you currently strengthen your memory? Do you utilize any memory-retrieval techniques? What jingles, rhymes, acrostics, or acronyms have you used over the years to remember things? How might you improve on some of the memory strategies you are already using? What additional strategies would you like to incorporate?

Chapter Recollections

- How do mnemonics work to improve your memory?

- How does a positive attitude help when learning and encoding complex information?

- What is the BEM Principle; and what does it tell us about the way we learn and remember?

- What is chunking; and how does this method improve recall?

- What role do emotions play when forming a memory?

- How does adequate sleep help maintain or strengthen memory? What role does REM sleep play in the memory process?

- How does the loci method trigger your memory? How is it different from the peg-word system?

- What kinds of memory tasks are best aided by the keyword method?

- Think about a typical trip for you to the grocery store: How might you apply the linking method so that you don't have to worry about forgetting anything or writing out a list?

- What acronyms to you use regularly?

- Do you remember learning any acrostics to aid your memory as a youngster?

- What rhymes or jingles have helped your memory in the past?

Amazing Applications for School Success

Will Memory Strategies Help Me Succeed in School?

In the school environment, we must contend with multiple learning goals and agendas which are often in competition for our time. First, there's the learning that you desire because you're curious and you find the subject meaningful. Then there's the curriculum your teacher wishes to impart. Then there's bureaucratic and parental expectations. Additionally, a student must learn what they'll be tested on. The subject of testing brings up another consideration. Some tests measure your knowledge, others your skills. Some may ask you to analyze a case-study, others require you to know a formula. Where one test may reward you for improvisational thinking and creativity, another will reward you for following directions. However much at odds the learning goals and testing approaches are—whether an essay exam, multiple-choice quiz, mathematical equation, oral presentation, or case study—they all have something in common. Each of them requires knowledge; and your knowledge is dependent upon your memory.

To ensure that you possess the requisite knowledge for school success, whatever the learning task may be, we recommend that you utilize all of the memory tools at your disposal. This chapter, therefore, outlines how the principles presented in Chapter 3 can be applied for optimal school success. Just as no single tool (like a saw) can be used to build a house, no single tool (like the linking method) can be used to meet all of your memory needs. As you become comfortable with all of the strategies outlined in *The Great Memory Book*, however, your memory tool chest will see you through the most taxing of learning situations.

Does Learning Mnemonics Undermine an In-depth Education?

Learning a system of MNEMONICS by no means replaces learning itself. It is rather an adjunct to learning. Like a computer, mnemonics provides a vehicle for shortening the path to mastery. It is with the aid of our tools, not the tools themselves, that we become educationally competent. Once students become efficient in the use of mnemonic tools, they can maximize their learning time. Competing agendas will become less of an issue as basic requirements are able to be met, with time to spare for

> *An object once attended to will remain in memory, whereas one inattentively allowed to pass will leave no traces.*
>
> —William James

the more personalized curriculum. A book published by the U.S. Department of Education, called *What Works* (1989), concludes that "Mnemonics help students remember more information faster and retain it longer."

New Jersey senator (1979-1997) Bill Bradley, known as one of the most intellectual and deep-thinking members of the United States Senate, would likely agree with the Department of Education's report. It is no coincidence that this Princeton graduate is also known as a memory expert. Bradley's memory skills enabled him to spend much less time doing schoolwork, leaving more time to reach his personal goals. This chapter prepares you, too, for the kind of school and professional success Bill Bradley has enjoyed.

What Memory Strategies Will Enhance My School Success?

Do you remember what three basic elements are involved in the memory process? Here's a quick review. For any new learning to stick, it must be:

- **Encoded (recorded);**
- **Maintained or strengthened (stored);**
- **Retrieved through association (recalled).**

The school success strategies that will enable you to master both your required and your desired learning in a time-efficient manner are encompassed in these three basic memory stages.

■ 9 School Success Strategies for Optimal Memory Encoding

1

Keep Your Cool
Pump yourself up with positive self-talk! Believe in your ability to master new things. Remind yourself that you can do it. If you get overwhelmed, refrain from making any long-term decisions or rash judgments about yourself as a learner. Instead, do something physically active; change the pace momentarily. Also, give yourself positive affirmations like, Mastery is easy; or My success is absolutely assured; or I have a great memory.

2

Learning Takes Energy
Make sure that you're alert for class and study time. Get plenty of uninterrupted sleep (6-8 hours); eat a high-protein breakfast; and if you're a coffee, coke, or tea drinker, limit your caffeine consumption or stick with decaf. Too much caffeine can reduce concentration and result in more mistakes. The ideal state for learning is alert—not hyper. A better alternative is physical exercise, which increases blood flow and oxygen delivery to your brain, thus increasing alertness.

3

Goal Seekers Are High Scorers
Make sure you know what you want to learn and why. Review the assignment and form a plan of attack. Write down your learning goals for the week, month, or term. Break them down into measurable steps, checkpoints, or objectives you can review often. Ideally, your goals will be balanced between what you are required to learn and what you wish to learn. The more these competing demands cross over, the better.

4

Get Proactive
Apply mnemonic principles introduced in Chapter 3 as you study. Encoding a memory can be as simple as pausing and thinking about how the new material you're learning relates to what you already know. Or, it can be more complex, like associating the material you're learning with places or parts of your body (loci).

5

Feed Your Memory Well
Your memory relies on vital nutrients to function optimally. You can ensure your brain receives adequate nourishment by maintaining a healthful diet

with plenty of fresh fruits, vegetables, and whole grains. You may also wish to consider how dietary supplements may improve your vitality and cognitive function (see Chapter 6 for more on memory nutrients).

6 Attend to the Middle

We know that the recalling sequence for most material is beginning, end, middle—that is, material presented at the beginning and end of a learning session will be better remembered than that presented in the middle. Known as the BEM principle, you can offset this effect by consciously paying more attention to the middle of the information block. Since you'll naturally remember the first and last blocks, a little extra effort applied to the middle will shore up the weak link.

7 Get Engaged First

Active engagement with the material ensures deeper understanding. Thus, ask yourself questions to bring the big picture into clear focus: What does this have to do with what we learned yesterday? What's coming up next? Why this and not that? Or, What exactly does this mean? The inquiry process is vital to the encoding and strengthening of memory. Ask questions in class. Double

check what you've learned with others. Seek feedback immediately, if possible, before any false impressions are formed.

8 Let's Party

Celebrate your learning. When strong emotions are present, the experience is more likely to get deeply imprinted in your memory. Excitement, humor, celebration, fear, pride, suspense, and other intense emotions stimulate the brain's production of NORADRENALINE, a potent memory-enhancing hormone, which mobilizes the mind and body for action. The release of this and other potent brain chemicals help serve as a biochemical marker, of sorts, making retrieval of the information more likely.

9 Picture Perfect

Visualize words into pictures. Make mind-maps to ensure that you are understanding the material, especially when it is being presented verbally. Mind-maps provide a visual, graphically organized pattern of what you're learning, which helps you encode, strengthen, and later retrieve the information. Making a mind-map is enjoyable and can be accomplished in the following four simple steps:

Steps for Mind-Mapping

1. Gather a large sheet of paper and some colored marking pens.
2. Write, draw, or otherwise depict the central topic on your paper.
3. Add branches radiating out from the main concept and label them with key ideas or perceptions. Add sub-branches to represent related ideas.
4. Personalize with colorful details—connecting lines, doodles, illustrations, symbols—all which help fix the concepts in your mind and stimulate later recall.

Figure 4.1

The following mind-map example illustrates how one's perceptions and understanding of a subject—in this case, the contents of this chapter—can be organized in a graphic visual manner; thus, increasing the chance of deeply encoding a complex topic.

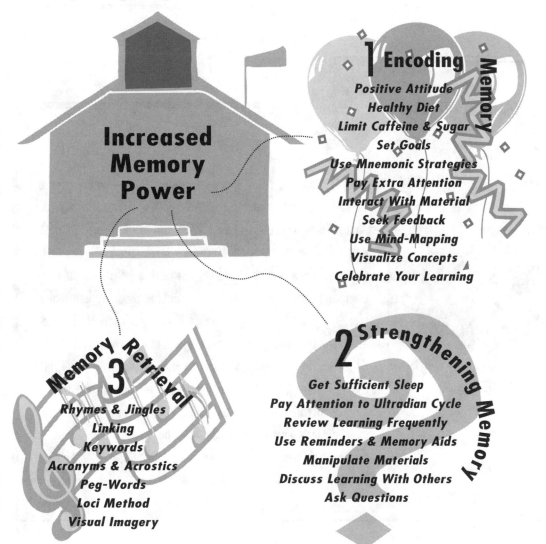

Memory Booster
Mind-Map Your Learning

Now it's your turn to design a mind-map. Pick your own topic, or if you'd rather, depict how the memory techniques you're learning right now might be used to enhance your school success. What subjects might you want to concentrate on first? What specific techniques could apply to these areas? Are there other areas of your life where you might benefit from using some of the strategies outlined thus far? What are they? For a reminder of the four simple steps involved in the making of a mind-map, turn back to page 65.

Case Study
Kindergartners Learn Calculus

Japanese educator Masachika Nakane developed a curriculum that included mathematics, science, spelling, grammar, and English—all based on extensive use of mnemonics such as stories, rhymes, and songs. Results of his efforts suggest that children as young as kindergarten can learn to perform math-

ematical operations with fractions, solve algebraic problems (including the use of the quadratic formula), generate formulas for chemical compounds, do elementary calculus, diagram their molecular structure, and learn a foreign language. Some of Nakane's mnemonics for basic mathematical computations have been adapted for use in the United States. One study found that third-grade children using these mnemonic strategies learned all the mathematical operations done with fractions in three hours. Beyond that, their mastery level (achieved in three *hours*) was comparable to that of sixth-graders who had received three *years* of traditional instruction in the subject (Higbee 1996).

6 School Success Strategies for Strengthening Your Memory

1 Sweet Dreams

Studies have shown that students who get sufficient sleep, but are deprived of their usual dream time do worse on logic and problem-solving tests than when their dream state is not interrupted. This suggests that it is not just sleep that is important to the memory process; dreaming is, as well. In fact, the more you learn during the day, the more time at night you're likely to spend dreaming. The dream state or REM (rapid eye movement) time consumes as much as 25 percent of our entire night's sleep and is critical to maintaining our memories (Hobson 1988). Earlier in the night, a smaller percentage of our sleep time is spent in REM. But as morning approaches, a large portion of our sleep time is spent dreaming. This suggests that the last few hours of sleep may be the most critical for the consolidation of learning. If you have a job or class that forces you to get up at 5 a.m. each day, it may be negatively impacting your memory.

2 Catch the Crest

The brain is not designed to learn non-stop; it demands rest. In fact, as sort of a built-in rest mechanism, the brain alternates energy consumption between the left and right hemispheres every ninety minutes or so. This body/mind rhythm is called an ultradian cycle. As a result of this alternating activity-rest cycle, tasks that are related more to the left side of the brain (sequential learning, understanding language, computing, and judgment) may be easier for you during a time when the left hemisphere is operating at peak efficiency. And tasks that are related more to the right-brain (imaginative learning, spatial memory, recognizing faces, visualizing images, and reconstructing songs) may be easier for you when your right hemisphere is operating at peak efficiency. Learning periods need to be interspersed with breaks for processing the material. It is during downtime that the brain synthesizes the learning and taps into the inner wiring necessary for memory connectivity and recall. Would you consider running a 10-K race without resting afterwards? Since learning is a biological process that literally changes the brain's configuration—making new synaptic connections and strengthening well-used ones—rest is also essential to optimal brain functioning. Thus, studying in forty-five- to ninety-minute segments with a fifteen-minute break in between increases learning efficiency since our daily highs and lows run about forty-five minutes apart. As you become familiar with your own ultradian rhythm, you can optimize your learning sessions by applying maximum energy during high-energy peaks and resting during low-energy dips.

Figure 4.2 below illustrates how time of day affects our ultradian rhythms, depicted here by the varying levels of brain wave activity, from beta to delta.

Figure 4.2

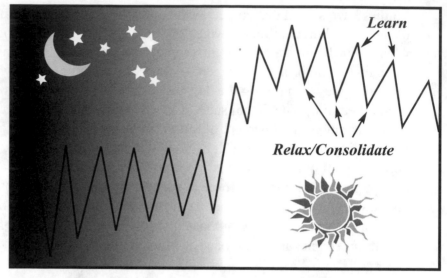

Beta
(Intense mental activity or normal arousal)

Alpha
(Brain at rest or meditative state)

Theta
(Deep reverie or drowsiness)

Delta
(Sleeping)

Learn

Relax/Consolidate

← Nighttime ·········· Daytime ········ →

3 **Repeat That Please**
The connection that is made between brain cells upon learning something new is strengthened with repetition. To ensure a strong connection, new material should be repeated within ten minutes after learning it, again within forty-eight hours and, if possible, after seven days. If you don't review what you've learned, you may be surprised to find at an inopportune time that the material—even though you distinctly remember learning it—has suddenly "skipped your mind." To review new learning, organize a study session with another student or group of students, reread your notes, and/or reread the first and last paragraphs of each page you're responsible for knowing. Creating a crossword puzzle is another enjoyable and creative review strategy. Others include watching a video on the subject, making a rap song utilizing the new concepts, or designing flashcards.

As with any new learning task, the real question is not whether you can succeed at it, but whether you are prepared to commit the necessary time and effort to succeed at it.

—Author Unknown

Where's Your Back Up?

As much as possible, back up your memory with "hard copies" or external memory aids—especially during high-stress periods when you may be juggling a lot of balls at one time. Get in the habit of carrying a calendar or personal notebook and be fanatic about writing in it. Use post-it notes, planning software (if you use a computer), an organized filing system, everyday objects, and even events to trigger your memory. No one's memory is perfect; and the more stress we're under, the more likely information floats by us without getting encoded. Backing up your personal memory system, like you back up your computer's memory system, just makes good sense.

An Hour-a-Day

Since humans are creatures of habit, the smartest thing we can do is take advantage of this tendency. Set aside time each day for practicing, reciting, and reviewing what you've learned. The evidence is very strong that learning in small daily chunks (interval learning) is far superior to "cramming" your head full of new information in one long sitting. Take a three-hour task and ask yourself, "How can I get the most out of my brain with the least effort?" Dividing the task down into forty-five-minute sessions over four days will give your brain the downtime it needs to consolidate the learning. Of course this method may take more discipline at first, but once you establish your hour-a-day routine, the learning advantage will become obvious and the process automatic.

> *Memory is like a piece of music—it has lots of different parts that come together to create the whole.*
>
> —Marcus Raichle

Say What?

The more you manipulate new information and verbalize it (active learning), the deeper your understanding of it will be. Mind-map what you're learning in a notebook, debate the subject in small groups, experiment with it, write about it, perform a skit about it, or verbalize it with accompanying body movements or hand motions. Find a study buddy and have weekly reviews. Look up the subject at the library and discover how many books have been written about it. There are hundreds of ways to manipulate materials for learning. Just walk into a "toy" or knowledge store and see for yourself. Or better yet, observe a toddler with a bowl of cereal at breakfast time doing everything with it imaginable, but eating it. This is how we learn best. When cold milk drips down a baby's face after dumping the bowl over his head you can be certain he'll remember the properties of milk.

Memory Workout
Test Your Observation Skills

Examine this picture carefully for a few minutes; then cover the page and record as many things about it as you can from memory.

Artist: Grandpa Bob Bates©

How many elements of the picture did you recall? What observation techniques did you use, if any? Do you want to improve your observation skills? If so, re-examine the image using the tips on the following page. Precise observation plays an integral role in the encoding of memory.

Sensory and Emotional Aspects:

■ Consider what general emotions or impressions the image evokes for you?

■ What aspects of the scene are most apparent; or require closer observation?

■ What personal meaning does the image hold for you? Does it remind you of anything in particular?

■ What would you hear, taste, smell, and feel if the scene were to come alive?

Cognitive Aspects:

■ What messages do you think the artist might be conveying?

■ What is the style of this artist? What makes the work original? How is it similar to other styles you've seen?

■ What period of time do you think the artist is depicting?

■ What objects appear in the foreground? What about the background?

Visual Training:

■ Move your eyes slowly in a structured way over the painting—from left to right, from top to bottom, and back again. Keep track of what you see.

■ Close your eyes and recall as clearly as possible the scene you just examined. What objects were in the left-top corner of the picture? How about the left-bottom, middle, right-top, and right-bottom portions?

■ Open your eyes and look again at the picture. How successful were you? What objects or details did you leave out or remember inaccurately?

This basic method of observation can be applied to anything you wish to remember. To practice your observation skills choose scenes or images at random and observe them carefully. Ask yourself the kinds of questions listed above. Then later, attempt to describe or depict what you observed. This can be done by writing about the scene or drawing it. As you make a habit of paying more attention to things around you and noticing the details of everyday life, your memory will improve, and likely your creativity and art skills, as well.

■ How Did You Do?

Which of the following twenty-one elements included in the preceding image were you able to remember? Did your recall improve the second time around?

Church	Pier	Family Picnic
Lake	Couple on the Pier	Horse Tied Up
2 Sailboats	Gazebo	Kids with Kite
Rowboat	Band in the Gazebo	Man and Bicycle
House on the Hill	Kid in Tree	Forest of Trees
Kids Running	Drug Store	First Horse and Buggy
Ice Cream Parlor	Birds in the Sky	Second Horse and Buggy

Mnemonic Tools for Memory Retrieval

A substantial amount of research published since the late 1970s has shown that mnemonics can help us with the kinds of learning tasks most often required in school (Higbee 1996). Since different mnemonic strategies work best for retrieving different types of material, we can't claim "one size fits all." Rather, you must decide which strategy works best for you and is most effective for the type of learning task you're attempting. On the following pages, we've provided a few examples of how various learning tasks can be aided by the mnemonic tools introduced in Chapter 3. Included in each section is an opportunity for you to interact with the material and try out the techniques for yourself.

■ Spelling and Vocabulary

Sound-Alike Words, Rhymes, and Linking - Choose pictures or images that represent the particular word or letter combination that you want to remember. Link the images together to form a story. Examples include: Bad gram***mar*** will ***mar*** a report; He screamed "***eee***" as he passed by the c***e***m***e***t***e***ry; The princi***pal*** is my ***pal***; A ***prize*** I will not win if I spell sur***prise*** like prize; Before I can fill a ***pre***scription, the doctor must ***pre***-authorize it; and, Before giving ***birth***, women are quite large in ***girth***.

"A lazy dude with lassitude."
Lassitude (LAS uh tood) listlessness, weariness. *Link: Lazy Dude*
Source: Vocabulary Cartoons™ (see Appendix)

Your Turn - Can you devise a mnemonic to remember the correct spelling or definition of each of the following words?

Millennium, Exacerbated, Bustle, Jaundice, Jalapeno, Ascension, Sensible

■ Public Speaking

Loci Method - To cue your memory for a series of key points, such as in an oral presentation, associate each point you want to make with a familiar set of loci (locations) occurring in a natural sequence (i.e., rooms in your house or body parts). For example, you might associate the introduction with the front door of your house (or top of your head); then, point 1 to your entryway (or neck), point 2 to your living room (or shoulders), and point 3 to your kitchen (or chest), etc.

Your Turn - Think of a joke you really want to remember. Now break it up into its key elements and associate each of these elements to a loci of your choice.

■ Classifying and Organizing Information

Peg-Words, Keywords, and Linking - These combined systems have helped students learn innumerable facts and figures, including, for example, the names (in order) of all the U.S. presidents. Here's how it works: 1) Use peg-words to represent the numbers one to ten, which will be used to remember the succession of the presidents; 2) Substitute sound-alike words for the Presidents' names; and 3) Link the two with a visual association, i.e., Tyler (tie), 10 (hen) = a hen wearing a tie to cue the memory that John Tyler was the tenth president. As you get into the larger numbers, combine pegwords (i.e., 14 might be a hen on top of a door). To remember state capitals identify sound-alike words and link them with visual imagery, (i.e., Indianapolis = An Indian juggling apples; or Boise, Idaho = a group of boys hoeing a potato patch). Consider this example for recalling the key topics presented in your biology textbook: Chapter 1: Introduction to Biology (1 = peg-word sun) - See the sun with a hat ***introducing*** itself to a snail; Chapter 2: The Circulatory System (2 = peg-word legs) - See a pair of legs with a ***blood***-red tattoo of a ***heart*** and ***lungs*** on them; Chapter 3: The Skeletal System (3 = peg-word bears) - See ***x-rays*** of The Three Little Bears; Chapter 4: The Nervous System (4 = peg: wheels) - See a huge ***nerve*** being wheeled into an operating room on a gurney; and so on.

Acronyms - ***CANU*** for example, can help learners remember which four Western states are the only ones in the country to meet at a single point: **C**olorado, **A**rizona, **N**evada, **U**tah.

Rhymes and Jingles - Most of us have learned more than we realize with the aid of jingles and rhymes. For example, we may recall the number of days in each month through the ditty, "Thirty days hath September, April, June, and November; When short February is done, all the rest have thirty-one."

Your Turn - What techniques might you incorporate to remember the five largest seas in the world (in order of size in square miles): ***Coral Sea*** (1,850,200 sq. miles), ***Arabian Sea*** (1,492,000 sq. miles), ***S. China (Nan) Sea*** (1,423,000 sq. miles), ***Caribbean Sea*** (971,000 sq. miles), ***Mediterranean Sea*** (967,000 sq. miles)

■ Medical Terms and Facts

Acronyms and Acrostics - For decades medical students have used acronyms, for example, ***NAVAL*** to remember the physiology of the leg in a proper order: **N**erve, **A**rtery, **V**ein, **A**nd **L**ymphatic system; or acrostics like "**O**n **O**ld **O**lympus' **T**owering **T**op **A** **F**inn **A**nd **G**erman **V**iewed **S**ome **H**ops" to remember the 12 cranial nerves: **O**lfactory, **O**ptic, **O**culomotor, **T**rochlear,

Trigeminal, Abducens, Facial, Auditory, Glossopharyngeal, Vagus, Spinal Accessory, and Hypoglossal.

Your Turn - Can you devise an acronym or acrostic to remember the four lobes of the CEREBRAL CORTEX: **Frontal**, **Parietal**, **Occipital**, and **Temporal**?

■ *Mathematical Concepts and Formulas*

Acrostics - The acrostic "**B**less **M**y **D**ear **A**unt **S**ally" has helped some math students learn the priority order of operations in an algebraic equation: **B**rackets, **M**ultiplication, **D**ivision, **A**ddition, and **S**ubtraction.

Peg-Words and Linking - Times-tables are easier for some people to remember when aided by the combined mnemonic techniques of peg-words and linking. First, the learner must know a peg-word system (2 = shoe, 4 = door, 8 = gate, etc.) Then when two numbers are multiplied, the peg-words are visualized interacting together. For example, you might visualize the equation 2 x 4 = 8 as follows: To save a friend, you kick down the door with your shoe, but now a gate blocks your entry.

Rhymes and Jingles - Those who might not otherwise remember the value of pi to 21 places may find it easier to remember the following ditty, "How I wish I could recapture pi. Eureka! cried the great inventor. Christmas pudding, Christmas pie is at the problem's very center." Can you guess how this strategy works? Each word in the jingle corresponds (by number of letters in it) to the next number in the pi sequence: 3.141592653589793223846 (i.e., 3 = how; 1 = I; 4 = wish). A teacher I knew told me the only way she eventually learned her times tables (in Junior High School) was when her remedial math teacher attached a rhyme to each equation (i.e., 6x4 is 24, shut the door and say no more).

Your Turn - Can you develop a mnemonic device to remember the following metric equivalencies? 1 inch = 2.54 cm, 1 foot = 30.48 cm, 1 yard = 0.9144 m, and 1 mile = 1.6093 km

■ *Foreign Language Vocabulary*

Keywords - The Japanese word for "You're welcome", pronounced "do eTASHeMASHta" sounds like the English phrase, "Don't touch the mustache." Any vocabulary word can be remembered by using this technique. Break the word down into syllables, then create a word or phrase that either sounds like the word you want to remember or that can be imagined in visual terms. The Hebrew word for good-night is "lilatov." When reduced to its two syllables, the word can be cued into your memory as lullaby (lila) time (tov).

Acronym - The acronym "MRS. VANDERTAMP" has been used to help French students remember most of the verbs that are conjugated with the helping verb "to be": Monter, Rester, Sortir, Venir, Aller, Naitre, Desendre, Entrer, Rentrer, Tomber, Arriver, Mourir, and Partir.

Your Turn - What strategy might you use to remember the following Spanish phrase: "Yo te quiero con todo mi corazon," which means I love you with all my heart.

■ *Reading and Comprehension*

Visual Imagery - When reading, visualize yourself saying what you are reading to an audience. This technique helps you to stay mentally focused. When you come to material that is difficult to understand, imagine yourself as a student asking for clarification or rephrasing the material to make sure you've understood it. Jot down notes in your mind's eye. Form mental pictures of key points and link them in ludicrous (memorable) images that form a story.

Your Turn - As you read the following Memory-Enhancing Study Tips, imagine you're a teacher reading the list to a classroom of students. Think about how you might help them to remember all thirteen tips.

Once you have mastered the basic mnemonic techniques described in Chapters 3, 4, and 5, you may wish to learn advanced mnemonic techniques. If so, you may find the "Suggestions for Further Study" in the appendix helpful.

Memory-Enhancing Study Tips

- **Make a realistic commitment to studying; create a timetable for yourself and stick to it until it becomes a habit.**

- **Divide the learning into short chunks of time followed by some downtime after each study session; avoid all-night cramming. You'll learn more in fifteen minutes of concentrated study than in sixty minutes of distracted study.**

- **Recall is naturally highest at the beginning and end of a session, so pay particular attention to the middle of a lecture, chapter, or paragraph. Many textbooks are written with this principle in mind.**

- **Practice using the mnemonic tools outlined in Chapters 3, 4, and 5.**

- Make sure that you're not hungry when you sit down to study; but also avoid a high-carbohydrate meal just beforehand. A good pre-study session meal is high in protein, but overall moderate calories.

- Since learning is enhanced when you're relaxed, take some time before you start studying to stretch, walk, or meditate—whatever relaxation techniques work best for you.

- Study in a comfortable space with good natural lighting (if possible).

- If you're studying a new subject, do a survey of the topic first so you can see how the parts relate to the whole before diving in. If the assignment requires reading a textbook, for example, review the introduction, table of contents and chapter previews and summaries.

- Active learning helps sustain your concentration, so take notes, self-test, ask questions, make a crossword puzzle, meet with a study group, and highlight key points. Write a brief outline in your own words or make a mind-map of the most pertinent points. Learning through passive absorption is much slower and less interesting.

- To strengthen your memory of the material, ask yourself how it relates to prior learning; seek associations with information you've already committed to memory.

- If you're writing notes about the material, be sure to write them in your own words; in this way, you are assessing your own understanding of the concepts.

- Slow down when you come across material that is difficult; resist the temptation to give up. Instead, reread it, move on, and return to it later to see if it makes more sense subsequently.

- Review main concepts every ten minutes; then again after one day, and again after one week. The review process is extremely important for encoding information in long-term memory. For a reading review, reread first and last sentences in each section, as well as the table of contents, chapter summaries, etc. As you come across keywords, see if you can reconstruct from memory what you learned about them.

Chapter Recollections

- How does the use of mnemonics aid learning?

- What three basic elements are necessary for new learning to stick?

- Review the encoding strategies presented in the chapter: Which ones do you already use? Were there any new ideas you might incorporate?

- Review the memory strengthening strategies: Did you learn anything that might help you perform better in school? What?

- Why do you think developing your observation skills enhances your memory?

- How have the mnemonic strategies known as peg-words, keywords, and linking, helped students with their schoolwork?

- What mnemonic method is suggested for remembering the parts of a speech? How else might you use this tool?

- How have rhymes and jingles been used to help students remember key facts and figures?

- How have acrostics and acronyms been used by students to remember information related to subjects like spelling, geography, physiology, etc.?

- What strategy is suggested for enhancing your concentration and memory for reading material? Have you tried this method? Does it work for you?

- Create your own personal list of memory tips that you can use to boost your recall.

What's Ahead?

Everyday High-Performance Memory

Chapter 5

Why Is the Subject of Memory Receiving So Much Attention These Days?

As the technological revolution seeps deeper into the fabric of our society, our memory systems are being challenged to meet the ever-increasing rate of change. What this means to the average person is that we are faced with the task of remembering more bits (and bytes) of information than ever before—from calling card numbers, ATM codes, and the mechanics of multiple communication systems to an entirely new vernacular that defines the latest technology. To keep up, we must be able to process a great quantity of information quickly and efficiently; and as important, we must be able to *remember* it.

The most successful people in the twenty-first century will be those who have learned ways to encode and recall the mass of information they deem important. Thus, in addition to physical fitness, high-achievers are beginning to realize the importance of mental fitness. This chapter provides a system for fine-tuning your memory system for everyday high-performance using the tools introduced in Chapter 3. The techniques we present are simple, practical, and easy to implement. They don't need to be complicated to work. Even children can learn these techniques.

Advanced mnemonic techniques based on the same principles have been presented by other authors. We've purposefully simplified the process because once you begin using them, you'll discover for yourself various additional purposes and approaches that will continue to improve your memory.

■ *Take Charge!*

A Cambridge University study directed by John Harris probed the methods people use for everyday remembering. The subjects were interviewed regarding their specific memory habits. They were asked such questions as, Do you use lists to run errands? Do you create rhymes or riddles to remember things? Do you use mental imagery? Do you use notes, pocket calendars, or day-timers?

The questions were designed to uncover two types of memory aids—"interior" or mental strategies and "exterior" or mechanical devices (see list below). The exterior aids (like lists and calendars) were found to be commonly used. But more surprising was the finding that interior strategies (like peg-words and linking) were virtually nonexistent! Most people simply don't take advantage of mnemonic strategies for increasing their recall. Perhaps if they learned them in school or if they knew how simple it can be to learn them, they would. The bottom line is this: If you want to have a high-performance memory system, get proactive. The few seconds that it takes to encode a memory can be the difference between forgetting and remembering.

Inside-Out Memory Aids

■ *"Interior" or Mental Memory Strategies*

- Sounding out the letters of the alphabet to inspire recall.
- Retracing one's steps or sequence of events to retrieve a forgotten cue.
- Rhymes or jingles: "Spring forward, fall back."
- Chunking: Remembering 74741295 as "a 747 for 12.95."
- Linking: Recalling lists by linking the items together with memorable associations.
- Story Linking: Creating a story to remember pieces of information.
- Peg-Word: Associating information with pre-established words and images.
- Keywords and sound-alike words: Visualizing a pair of ducks to remember the word *paradox*, or a girl tracing a star to remember the name Tracy Starr.
- Loci: Associating information with a pre-established set of familiar locations ordered in a logical fashion (i.e., body parts).

- Acronyms and acrostics: Associating key concepts with abbreviations or words that begin with the same letter: HOMES to remember the five Great Lakes; and "Every Good Boy Does Fine" to remember the notes on the treble clef.
- Elaboration or association with prior learning: Remembering that Montgomery is the capital of Alabama by associating it with the civil-rights/civil-disobedience acts of the 1960s.

"Exterior" or Mechanical Memory Devices

- Written lists, notes, and outlines
- Journal or diary entries
- Calendars, agendas, or Daytimers
- Alarm clocks or timers
- Tying a string around the finger
- Posting a visual cue
- Asking another person to remind you
- Prominent placement of something
- Mind-maps
- Answering machines and electronic message devices
- Photographs, scrapbooks, and videos

Get Mnemonicized!

It is infinitely easier to remember things that are cued or encoded into your memory with a mnemonic. Like planting flowers in the spring, you can be certain when you plant a memory cue that your summer garden will be satisfying. All of the mnemonic tools introduced in Chapter 3: Loci, Peg-words, Linking, Keywords, Acronyms, Acrostics, and Rhymes and Jingles, work because they provide the brain with a potent cue for remembering a chunk of information. The general memory-strengthening strategies presented in Chapters 3 and 4—from Precise Observation to Forming Habits—work because they encourage you to pay attention, take care of your body, and tune into the way your brain processes information.

I had banished every memory that you and I had ever made... But when you touch me like this...and I kiss you like that... It was so long ago but it's all coming back to me now.

—Celine Dion

Case Study
Get the Connection

A simple experiment conducted by researchers at Vanderbilt University in Tennessee demonstrates how much easier it is to learn information when it can be linked to existing knowledge. A group of students were asked to listen to ten simple insignificant sentences similar to the following:

The funny man bought a ring. The bald man read the newspaper. The attractive woman wore earrings. Afterward, the students were tested on the information which revealed, on average, 40 percent correct answers. Another group of students listened to the same sentences, only a few more details were added, such as: The funny man bought a ring that squirted water. The bald man read the newspaper to look for a hat sale. The attractive woman wore earrings she found in the trash bin.

This group of students was given the same test as the first group; and surprisingly, their performance was better. Although, the second group had to listen to longer sentences, they remembered considerably more—70 percent.

Researchers point out that when we are able to make memorable connections between chunks of information—that is, linking them to something we already know and noticing congruencies or incongruencies—the information is more likely to be recalled. In this case, what the students knew, for example, about the relationship between baldness and hats, or a "funny" man with a silly ring, or the incongruency of an attractive woman looking through the trash bin, created a stronger, more memorable association and visual image.

Is It Really Possible to Improve My Memory for Numbers?

Studies suggest that the answer to this question is yes. One study conducted by Carnegie-Mellon University demonstrated that a person can, indeed, improve their recall of random numbers with practice. At the onset of the experiment, the subject—an average student—could recall up to six digits at a time. After practicing for a couple of weeks he improved to some degree, and by the end of the experiment—18 months later—he could repeat back to the researcher a list of up to 84 digits. Guess how he accomplished the task. You've got it—by associating the numbers (after chunking them down) to his pre-existing knowledge base—in this case to race times as he was an avid cross-country runner. The student's memory improvement was not a result of mere practice or "exercise," note researchers: The key to his success was his ability to cue the numbers into a meaningful pattern through association.

Everyone's life is full of significant numbers. Think about particular numbers that are meaningful to you. Once you identify them, start using them for memory-association purposes. Pretty soon you'll find yourself using this simple technique everyday. The following examples are significant numbers you have probably already committed to memory.

■ *Significant Numbers*

- ■ Birthdays (yours, your spouse's, best friend's, children's, relatives')
- ■ Anniversaries (yours, your parent's, your siblings', etc.)
- ■ Significant years (high school graduation, death of a loved one, professional achievements, wars, dates in history, etc.)
- ■ Golf scores, bowling scores, or other numbers related to a favorite sport
- ■ Driver's license number
- ■ Social security number
- ■ Checking account number
- ■ ATM password or security code
- ■ License plate number
- ■ Your lucky number(s)
- ■ Highway or interstate numbers
- ■ Sports statistics (player stats, game scores, home runs, years, averages)
- ■ Numbers associated with a hobby or collection you have (antiques, coins, butterflies, etc.)
- ■ Lock combinations
- ■ Street addresses, zip codes, and phone numbers

Practice using both single and various number combinations previously committed to memory for making a quick association with new numbers. The more you depend on this system, the more automatic and dependable it becomes. What you are doing is replacing an abstraction with something meaningful. If it is a long number set, break it up into smaller chunks of four or less. For example, the 11-digit number, 10159711100, when chunked and cued might become, "Highway 101 meets Interstate 5, 9 miles into the route, after passing a 7-11 and 100s of stop signs." Phone numbers follow the rule by breaking the 10-digit number into three smaller chunks: area code, prefix, and last four digits. Banks and government entities have relied on this memory trick forever. You can too!

■ *Turning Numbers Into Objects*

If you're like me, you remember concrete objects and images better than numbers; they're simply more meaningful to you. This is not uncommon, nor is it bad. It means that you're probably a visually-dominant learner—that is, your memory is best encoded through visual images. If you're more inclined to remember information in visual terms, you'll naturally create associations that form a storyline as we did in the previous example. If you're more inclined to remember information in auditory/verbal terms, however, you'll naturally create sound-alike associations, like riddles, puns, and rhymes.

The peg-word system works by "coding" numbers with something more concrete, like objects. As described in Chapter 3, this system requires an initial investment of time as you memorize a particular word to represent each number; however, once you've done that, peg-words can be used for a host of memory tasks. If you memorize ten numbers, you can combine images to represent quantities greater than ten. Whatever peg-words make sense to you are the best ones to use. Many people (usually auditory/verbal learners) prefer to use rhyming peg-words such as those identified in the familiar nursery rhyme, "One-Two Buckle My Shoe" (see list below). Others (usually visual learners) find shape associations easier to remember (also listed below).

Rhyming Peg-Words	*Shape Associations*
Zero..........................Hero	Zero..........................A ball
One............................Bun	One........................A pencil
Two...........................Shoe	Two...........................A swan
Three.........................Tree	Three...Double golden arches
Four........................Door	Four......................A pennant
Five...........................Hive	Five...........................A snake
Six............................Sticks	Six..................A mouse with
Seven.....................Heaven	a long tail
Eight.......................Gate	Seven..........................A cliff
Nine.......................Sign	Eight.................A snowman
Ten.........................Hen	Nine...................A balloon

Using a combined approach of peg-words and linking, an otherwise insignificant 11-digit number, like 01540198136, can be visually encoded. Consider, for the sake of example, this silly association: "The *hero* was eating a hamburger *bun* stacked full like a bee *hive*. He ate so much he couldn't fit through the *door*, so he ceased to be my *hero*. I couldn't bear to look at a *bun* again without seeing a *sign* in my mind of a *gate* and a *bun* too fat to fit through it. The only way I could escape the thought was to climb a *tree* and imagine myself as a *stick*."

The above association is indeed cumbersome; so how might you make the process more efficient? Upon chunking the number down to a more manageable size, you might end up with something like, "My hero was born in 1540 and though I didn't learn about her until 1981, she represents an important branch on my learning tree."

When the memory task at hand calls for remembering a series of combined letters and numbers, simply apply multiple mnemonic techniques. Let's say, for example, you want to replace your old vacuum bags, and their package code is MT40911164W. A simple and powerful cue can be formed by encoding the letters with an acronym and the numbers with any combination of number strategies. The following example illustrates how a combined mnemonic approach can simplify the encoding task. In this case, the five techniques utilized are: chunking, acronyms, meaningful number associations, sound-alike words, and linking.

Combined Mnemonic Techniques

MT............................	My TransAm
409..........................	(engine size)... is so fast it will
111..........................	win, win, win (one, one, one)
6...............................	six races
4...............................	for
W.............................	washing (it)

When strung together, they form the simple sentence: "My TransAm 409 is so fast it will win, win, win six races just for washing it." With a little imagination, you'll find a zillion associations and feel like a memory wizard!

Memory Booster
The Road-Trip Mnemonics Game

Try it yourself; make it a game. The next long drive with the kids is a perfect time to introduce this MNEMONIC technique to the whole family. Children as young as age four have been able to learn and utilize these simple techniques. The game goes like this: Somebody starts by selecting a license plate from a passing car and applying a mnemonic strategy to remember it. This can also be done simultaneously by all players. One player than verbalizes their cue. The next player has to recite the cue of the player prior to them and then their own. Each person gets a turn until returning to the first player, who tries to recite the whole string of cues. On the trip home, test each other's long-term memory. Can you still visualize the associations you formed hours or days ago? If so, you have learned to effectively cue your memory for numbers.

Memory Booster
Nimble Number Associations

Below is a sample list of 25 numbers containing just one of a thousand potential associations. Now, it's your turn to come up with a few of your own.

Our List:	Your List:
1 ....First place	_____
5 ....Quittin' time	_____
6 ....A six-pack	_____
7 ....Days in the week	_____
9 ....A cat's lives	_____
10 ....Your fingers	_____
12 ....Lunchtime	_____
13 ....A baker's dozen	_____
14 ....Valentine's Day	_____
15 ....Quinceañera	_____
16 ....Sweet sixteen	_____
21 ....Blackjack	_____
25 ....Christmas	_____
26 ....Miles in a marathon	_____
41 ....Attack on Pearl Harbor	_____
45 ....A right-angle	_____
50 ....Golden Anniversary	_____
52 ....Weeks in the year	_____
60 ....Beetle-mania	_____
70 ....A peace sign	_____
76 ....Declaration of Independence	_____
100 ....A century	_____
360 ....A circle	_____
365 ....Days in the year	_____

*W*ho's Who Among Memory Geniuses

A host of cases recorded in various source books reveal the scope and magnitude of our incredible human-memory potential. Here, we introduce you to ten of the most interesting memory geniuses of all time.

1   Conductor Arturo Toscanni is said to have known by heart every note of every instrument for 250 symphonic works, plus the words and music to 100 operas. At one concert, just as the orchestra was preparing to open, the second bassoonist discovered that a key on his instrument was broken. Upon hearing this, Toscanni paused deep in thought for a moment, then finally said, "It's all right. That note doesn't occur in tonight's concert."

2   Hideaki Tomoyori of Yokohama, Japan, recited from memory the mathematical value of pi to 40,000 decimal places breaking the previously recorded world-record of 10,000.

3   Antonio de Marco Magliabechi, an Italian born in 1633, used his incredible photographic memory and mastery of speed reading to demonstrate how he could write out the entire contents of a book after one reading.

4   Dario Donatelli, still living, broke the world's speed memorization record by accurately recalling a series of seventy-three numbers within forty-eight seconds of first hearing them. The previous world record was established in 1911 with a string of eighteen numbers.

5   Kaumatana, a Maori Chief from New Zealand, could recite from memory the entire history of his tribe, spanning forty-five generations and 1,000 years. Each recitation took three days.

6   Stephen Powelson, a retired accountant from Les-Loges-en-Josas, France memorized more than 14,300 lines of Homer's 15,693-line *Iliad* in classical Greek. The feat took Powelson about ten years to achieve; he started when he was sixty-years-old.

7   Telephone operator Gou Yanling memorized more than 15,000 telephone numbers in Harbin, China.

8   Cardinal Mezzofani spoke sixty languages, most of them fluently.

9 Christian Friedrich Hernaker, the infant genius of Lubeck, Germany, was born in 1721. By the age of ten months he could repeat every word spoken to him; by age three, he could speak Latin and French, and had a comprehensive knowledge of the bible, geography, and world history. Sadly, the boy genius died at the age of four following his own prediction of his death.

10 Reverend David Misenheimer of Charlotte, North Carolina is known for his ability to put names to faces. Each Sunday, he greets every person of his congregation—all 1,800 of them—by name as they enter the church. He says he's not really sure how he does it, but he can even remember the names of visitors who attended church one time six months previously.

Sources: *Guinness Book of World Records* (1996); *Brain Builders* (1995); *Maximum Brainpower* (1989); *Boost Your Brain Power* (1991); and *Committed To Memory* (1998).

What Memory Tricks Will Help Me Remember a List of Items?

Hopefully, we've convinced you that people can dramatically enhance their recall just by learning a few memory "tricks." If not, maybe the following findings will. Studies conducted at various universities around the world have generally concluded that people who are asked to memorize a thirty-item list without using any learning strategies are usually capable of recalling about ten items. The number increases, however, to twenty items (100% improvement) when the subjects are taught a few basic mnemonic strategies; and those using multiple strategies are able to memorize all of the items most of the time—a 150 percent increase. The following basic memory tricks, when combined with the rest of the strategies you're learning, can put you, too, into this peak-performance category.

Let's experiment! Start by giving yourself a few minutes to read and remember the following list of thirty items; however, don't use any of the mnemonic tools you've learned thus far (I know it is difficult not to). Then cover the words and write down as many as you can remember. Repeat the test again, but this time use whatever mnemonic strategy or combination of strategies you wish.

Coffee	*Water*	*Soap*
Milk	*Juice*	*Candles*
Bread	*Sour Cream*	*Sponges*
Avocado	*Lettuce*	*Oranges*
Eggs	*Tuna*	*Cottage Cheese*
Tomato Soup	*Sugar*	*Cotton*
Apples	*Cough Syrup*	*Soda*
Laundry Soap	*Flowers*	*Cheese*
Cereal	*Ground Beef*	*Celery*
Light Bulbs	*Notepad*	*Pencils*

How did you do? Are you convinced yet? Maybe this was easy for you; or maybe it wasn't. There are many strategies you can apply to improve your performance on a memory task of this nature. How many of the following tools did you find yourself using?

■ *Encode With Acrostics*

Make up a sentence that is silly or meaningful (and therefore, memorable) using the first letter of each word on the list. Let's use, for example, the letters from the items in the first row of the grocery list above, which are: C • M • B • A • E • TS • A • LS • C • LB. Try it for yourself.

The acrostic we formed is:
"**C**arl is pursuing an ***MBA*** in **E**astern **T**hought **S**tudies **A**t **L**ouisiana **S**tate **C**ollege where he also ***L**awn **B**owls."*

Once you've formed an acrostic, you have a starting place for memory retrieval: It narrows the field from all items stocked on the grocery store shelves to items you need and the letters they begin with. This technique should improve your recall to some degree; however, when incorporated with additional strategies, your memory will improve all the more. Keep reading.

■ *Arranging Lists by Category*

In the example above, the groceries were listed in random order; but how might the list be more logically organized? Consider how your local grocery store is laid out. In what section do you usually start your shopping? And how do you proceed through the store? Visualize yourself doing this for a moment. Now re-arrange the above list so that it is synchronized with your normal shopping routine. Applying an acrostic sentence to a logical order of items is much more efficient. If you want to remember, for instance, the planets within our solar system, create an order first (i.e., from the sun) and then apply the mnemonic. Of course, as you make a habit of relying on interior memory strategies rather than exterior strategies, you will get faster at encoding lists in this way.

◼ *Remembering Lists By Loci*

Another excellent mnemonic technique for organizing and encoding a list is the loci method. As you'll remember from Chapter 3, loci—meaning locations in Greek—operates on the same principle as the peg-word system—paired association. The association "pegs" you will use in the loci method, however, are locations rather than objects. The first step, therefore, is to create in your mind a framework of familiar locations which will become your loci. Many people visualize the rooms in their house for this purpose because usually our home is very familiar to us. However, any set of locations that you know well will work fine. Perhaps, for you it is the stores on Main Street, or your place of work, or parts of your body. Go ahead now and visualize six primary locations in a logical order—that is, the way you would likely encounter them. For example, the loci I most frequently use are the porch to my house, my entryway, the kitchen, the living room, the dining room, and the bathroom. The order in which you visualize the locations are important because it must remain the same each time you use them.

Once you are comfortable with the six primary loci-pegs you've selected, visualize four stable items or features found in each of these areas. For example, my porch pegs are the gate, stairs, bench, and door. Once you've identified pegs in each loci, you'll have the basis for a powerful memory tool. The next step, of course, is applying the method. Let's use the first row of the grocery list again for practice purposes. There are multiple ways in which the application of your loci can be approached. In example 1, each item is treated individually; and in example 2 the items are categorized first for efficiency.

Example 1

I open the **gate** to the **porch** and spill my **coffee**.
Milk is trickling down the **stairs**.
A loaf of **bread** is on the **bench**.
Avocado dip is squishing out of the keyhole in the **door**.
As I walk into the **entryway,** A crate of **eggs** is on the **window** sill.
A hot bowl of **tomato soup** sets on the **halltree** shelf.
I open the **coat closet** and a bushel of **apples** comes tumbling out.
I pass the **statue** in the hall and **laundry soap** is foaming up all around it.
I walk into the **kitchen** and the **sink** is full of **cereal**.
I open the **refrigerator** and wonder who in the world put a package of **light bulbs** on the shelf.

The key for success with the loci method is conjuring up a strong visual image for each thing you wish to remember while associating it with your pre-established loci pegs. For some memory tasks (especially long lists) you may find that it is more practical to categorize your list first and then apply the mnemonic. Using the same list of grocery items, we'll demonstrate this technique. Since all of the items I need will be stored in my kitchen, I can reduce the loci pegs to that room: and order them in a logical fashion (i.e., where the items are stored).

Example 2

Sink	Refrigerator	Pantry
Laundry Soap	*Milk*	*Coffee*
Light Bulbs	*Eggs*	*Bread*
	Avocado	*Tomato Soup*
	Apples	*Cereal*

Now it's your turn. As you link the items listed above to their respective loci pegs and each other, keep in mind the following tips for strong associations:

Remember when you form associations to...

- **Imagine each item as vividly as possible.**
- **Make sure the image is concrete—a noun.**
- **Create action.**
- **Make it bizarre.**
- **Make it personal to your life.**
- **Make it humorous.**
- **Ensure items are strongly linked together.**
- **Use pre-established peg-words or loci-pegs if possible.**

What Strategies Can I Use to Better Recall Names and Faces?

The basic principles underlying most memory enhancement strategies are virtually the same: attention, visual imagery, association with existing knowledge, synthesis of material, rehearsal, and organization. Remembering names and faces is no different. Simply proceed as follows:

■ *Your Attention Please*

The most important first step for remembering names and faces is acknowledging your desire to do so. Make a commitment to it. If you expect to be in a situation where you will be meeting many new people at once, see if you can obtain a list of names ahead of time. If you can, review the names and begin to form some immediate associations. If you're committed to recalling people's names and faces, your attention will be fixed on that goal. Blank looking rather than real seeing is one of the primary causes for poor memory. Don't expect to remember somebody's name if you don't make a point of it. When you meet a new person, listen and observe carefully. Engage your senses. Note what their most distinct feature is. And then elaborate.

■ *Your Mind's Eye*

Consider what meaning the person's name holds, or who you know by the same name, or how it sounds or looks. Then, transform the name into something concrete. Here are some simple examples:

- When the name is synonymous with a concrete object(s); i.e., Frank Ball, imagine eating franks at the ball park.
- When the name sounds like a concrete object(s); i.e., Dotty Weissberg, break it down and imagine a dotted iceberg.
- When the name includes an adjective; i.e., Bill Green, imagine that Bill is green with envy, or a green dollar bill.
- When the name reminds you of something concrete; i.e., Bob McDonald, imagine bobbing for hamburgers.
- When the name is synonymous with a location; i.e., Joe Montana, imagine a kangaroo living in Montana, or a joy-ride through Montana.
- When the name includes a common prefix or suffix; i.e., Karen Richard*son*, utilize pre-established symbols of your choice; for example, the sun shining down on a rich and caring person.
- When you notice a striking feature, incorporate it somehow into the visual; i.e., Kelly Beahl... looks good in high heels; or Verbose Carlos. This technique is most effective as a rhyme.

■ *Try It Yourself*

The visual connection you create must be strong enough that it will later trigger your memory.

James Colberg _____ Arturo Fernandez _____

Sandy Henderson _____ Mark Lindsey _____

Curtis Herschel _____ Howard Stefanoff _____

Michelle McCaffry _____ Alan Fiero _____

Jennifer Sayles _____ Lin Chang _____

*W*hat Do You Know?

As you listen to the sound of the person's name, associate it with someone or something previously stored in your memory. For example, when you are intro-duced to Hilary Wilson, you might think of Hilary Clinton meeting Dennis the Menace's neighbor, Mr. Wilson. Some names are more challenging than others, but don't get discour-aged in the process. The very act of considering an association deepens the memory trace. Some studies suggest that a person's name is more frequently remembered when it is offered two to four minutes after an initial introduction. This finding supports the concept that the more we know about somebody, the more potential associations exist.

A person's name is more often remembered when it's offered a few minutes following the ini-tial introduction. It is believed that the wider span of time sup-ports a deeper or more likely association.

■ *Repeat After Me*

If you forget a person's name, simply ask them to repeat it. Most people will be flattered that you care enough to make the request. Now rein-force their name in your memory by incorporating it into your conversation (i.e., "Tell me, Carol, what do you think about the situation?"). Or ask them how their name is spelled or where it originates. When you part company, repeat it again (i.e., "It was a pleasure meeting you, Tracy. I hope I'll see you later"). Then before you are swept into the next conversation, pause momentarily to review internally what facts you want to remember about the person. If you're meeting many people at one time, you may want to keep an index card in your pocket to write down names accompanied by the person's most distinctive feature.

■ *File What's Important*

Once you've committed to memory people's names and faces, now you need to encode where it was that you met them or other pertinent facts. To do this, syn-thesize your name cue with the additional information. For example, I want to remember that I met Katie Langston at the gym and that she likes going out for happy hour. Thus, I reinforce this information by visualizing a *caddie* carrying a *lanky* woman who appears to weigh a *ton*; she is wearing a *sweatsuit* and is passed out from having too much *fun*. Perhaps, this is not the most compli-mentary image, but it is likely a memorable one and it rhymes. If your visual imagery resembles mine, I suggest that you don't share the nature of it with the person when they inevitably ask, "How did you remember all that about me?"

To consider how well this system works, take a few moments to study each of the six names and faces below using the approach we've described. Remember to notice a dominant or striking feature; turn the name into a concrete object(s) or symbol(s); form a sound-alike cue; or consider who else you know by the same name; then link the associations together with an action-oriented visual or rhyme. Once you've done this, continue reading. Don't worry about trying to remember the names and faces once you've completed the exercise.

Carl Sandburg

Colette Carnegie

J.T. Kale

Liche Fuerte

Morgan Cummings

Lola Robertson

How Can I Help My Spouse (Parent, Child, or Partner) Be Less Absentminded?

The kind of forgetting that is usually attributed to "absentmindedness" is the easiest to remedy. The issue is often related to selective focusing—that is, like the "absentminded professor," the person only notices and cares about that which is related to their work. "It just skipped my mind," says the forgetful spouse who fails to call when delayed at the office. And yet we never "forget" to call our employer when we're delayed at home, right? This strange phenomenon of "selective memory" is really more related to perception of priorities than bad memory. Seeking commitment from the "forgetful" person, will be more productive than berating them.

■ Helping Children Remember

The teenager who forgets to take the trash out and the co-worker who forgets to complete an important task are no different. Remind them of their responsibility and work with them to adjust their priorities. Your young child, however, is a different story. Child development experts warn not to expect too much of your second grader's memory. Children have to learn how to remember things. Work with them to learn some simple strategies, such as associating the school bell with gathering their homework, lunchbox, and jacket in that order. Say to them, "When the bell rings to leave school, what three things do you need to do before starting home?" It's never too

Children have to learn how to remember things. Work with them to learn some simple memory techniques.

early to begin working with them in this manner. Children exhibit better short-term than long-term memory—a logical occurrence considering their short past. See "A Child's Developing Memory" on the following page.

■ Snapshot Memory

Everyday absentmindedness, like where you stored the birthday card you bought last month, where you parked your car at the mall, or where you put your keys, can be avoided simply by paying more attention. One memory technique that is easy to apply is to pretend you're taking a snapshot of the pertinent circumstance. Pause and freeze the moment. As you tuck the birthday card away in your desk drawer, hold your hands up to your eyes in the shape of a camera and click the visual cue right into your brain.

■ *Officer, Can You Help Me Find My Car?*

Parking garages almost always offer standard visual cues—usually in the form of brightly colored numbers or letters painted on columns, elevators, or signs. Once you notice that you are parked on level three, row D, you might, for example, visualize yourself wearing 3D-movie glasses. If the lot doesn't provide these obvious cues, take a moment and pretend you're explaining to a police officer where you think your car was parked. Just the process of imagining this scenario will prevent it from happening. Anything you do to sustain your attention and increase your observation skills is going to improve your memory. As for remembering where your keys are, if you get in the habit of putting them in the same place each time, your problem will be resolved.

Take an extra look around, make a nonsense association, verbalize the moment, visualize the consequences of forgetting, or recite the information a time or two. The few seconds that it takes to encode a memory is the difference between involuntary and voluntary forgetfulness. Move out of the passenger's seat and into the cockpit. With increased memory awareness you'll gain greater control. Superior recall is really no mystery! You don't have to buy it, find it, give up something for it, or stress over it. You just have to cue it.

A Child's Developing Memory

A baby is born with more brain cells than she or he will ever possess again. In fact, the critical first few years mark the most productive learning time in a person's life. Does this profound learning period so early in life mean that a baby has the ability to remember? Some scientists suspect that "memory" formation begins as early as in the womb. Others believe we really can't formulate memory until we've developed conceptual skills. Perhaps, the key is **how** *memory* is defined. The following examples reflect a newborn's **recognition** ability versus **recall**; but all the same, it may point to a primal prenatal memory of sorts.

Studies have demonstrated a newborn's ability to pick out their own mother's voice from a field of voices and to recognize unusual words (like *tinder* and *beguile*) after two weeks of "training," whereby the words were repeated to the infants ten times each, six times a day. In addition, one study found that infants "selected" a Dr. Seuss story read frequently to them while in the womb over one they had never heard before (see Chapter 7: You're Never Too Young to Be Primed). Could this explain a person's natural "ear" for particular selections of music or types of instruments? Thomas Verny, author of *The Secret Life of Your Unborn Child* (1981), relates the story of conductor Boris Brott of the Hamilton Ontario Symphony. Brott discovered as a young child that he could play certain complex pieces without "learning" them. His mother, a professional cellist, remembered that the pieces in question were ones she had practiced repeatedly during her pregnancy.

continued—

—continued

Other scholars believe, however, that most people can't "remember" anything before the age of two or three because infants (meaning "incapable of speech" in Latin) don't have the language to label and process an experience. If awareness is a necessary component of memory, this premise makes sense. A child must first learn about the outside world before they can mentally reproduce it. Without discriminatory awareness of themselves versus others, information is not likely to be processed in a memorable way. As such, the knowledge base required for anything more than rudimentary memory formation probably includes object properties, functional associations, cause and effect understanding, spatial awareness, and a basic sense of time. It is interesting to note that when most people are asked what their earliest memory is, it is common for it to have occurred around the age of three—the time when the HIPPOCAMPUS, the brain structure necessary for conscious memory, has fully developed. Remembered scenes before this age are typically photographic-like—rich in color and detail, but lacking context. As three-year-olds develop language command they begin to demonstrate some acquisition of "long-term" memory. A child's long-term memory (a relative term), however, will not be as operational as their short-term memory due to their underdeveloped sense of time and their lack of distant events to remember.

Since it's normal for children's cognitive development to fluctuate by up to three years, parents and teachers should remain patient and flexible, and watch for signs of mental readiness—a precursor to learning. When a child is ready, introducing strategies, such as rehearsing, classifying things into categories, suggesting solutions to real problems, making up mnemonic associations, and discussing how to remember things, can help them develop a sense of memory control. Teach children *how* to plant cues for recall (see Chapter 3: Mnemonics for Family Fun). Emphasize learning from past experiences. Engage them in puzzles, games (chess is excellent), and toys that emphasize matching, discovery, and recall. Attach rhymes to concepts you want them to remember. At this stage bringing a sense of joy to the learning process is very important. Remember that the older the child is, the more "chunks" of information they can handle (see Chapter 3: Chunk It).

Provide an enriched environment. The movie *The Dead Poet's Society* exemplifies how much environment can impact children's learning and memory. If you saw the movie, you will remember that there were many changes in location and circumstances; the children's emotions were engaged; movement and novelty were incorporated; and a true-life learning opportunity provided a deep sense of meaningfulness to the learning process. Of course, meaningfulness does not have to happen on a grand scale. As a personal example, I can still recite Max Ehermann's *Desiderata* from memory thanks to a challenge my Mother posed when I was no older than ten. When I asked her what she wanted for her birthday that year, her response was "for you to memorize the *Desiderata* for me." That was supposed to be my gift to her: As it turned out, it was her gift to me, as well. Teaching children to use their memory is a lesson that will serve them well—and well into their sunset years.

■ *Pen the Name on the Face*

Remember the exercise you did earlier in this chapter to encode names and faces into your memory? Here's your chance see how well it worked. Look at each of the six photographs below and notice what comes to mind. Does the person's dominant feature pop out at you? If so, the next cue (and their name) should follow.

If you have trouble *recalling* the names, see if you can *recognize* the correct match from the list on the following page. *Recognizing* is easier than *recalling* because a clue is usually enough to trigger the association. It gives us a starting place, rather than having to probe our entire memory for one. To strengthen your memory for names and faces, practice associating how the person looks (or their most distinctive feature) with a meaningful or concrete image that represents their name.

As you incorporate the strategies in this chapter to your day-to-day life, soon you'll be doing it automatically. As simply as you learned to ride a bike, you'll look back and wonder when it was exactly that you gained such good memory balance and dexterity for names and faces.

*C*hapter Recollections

- What is the difference between interior and exterior memory aids? Which do you rely on more?

- Why do you think it is easier to remember new information when you can link it to existing knowledge?

- What strategies did you learn for remembering numbers? What two key strategies did the runner in the Carnegie-Mellon study use?

- What type of peg-word system to you prefer? Do you think you're a more visual learner or auditory/verbal learner? Why?

- In what ways might you use your list of personally significant numbers to help you remember otherwise abstract information.

- When is it a good idea to use a combined mnemonic approach?

- What strategies did you learn for remembering lists?

- When is it a good idea to organize a list into a logical order or subcategories before applying the cue?

- What elements make for a strong and memorable association?

- What are the steps for remembering names and faces?

- What kinds of things can I look for in a name to help me make a strong association.

- What strategies did you learn to help yourself (or others) be less absentminded?

- What can we do to help children develop their memory?

- What distinction is important to make in the argument about how early children form memory?

Recognition List for "Pen the Name on the Face" Exercise (Page 98)
Now do you *recognize* who's who?
John Sanders, Liche Fuerte, Samson Adams, Carl Sandburg, Sonja Ortiz, Morgan Cummings, J.T. Kale, Lola Robertson, Henry Austin, D.K. Custer, Colette Carnegie

What's Ahead?

Nature's Own Memory Nutrients

Chapter 6

How Does Diet Impact Your Memory?

Through the ages, human beings have sought to find the glass slipper that would manifest in some magical fashion the full potential of human memory. The effort has not been completely unfruitful. The magic, although not found in the form of a shoe, has appeared in something just as common—the foods we eat. Research conducted in the areas of nutrition, medicine, natural healing, and the mind/body connection over the past few decades has confirmed the importance of diet to mental functioning. A growing base of research supports the claim that poor nutrition greatly impacts learning and memory. Beyond the obvious—that if you feel good, your concentration will be better—to function at optimal capacity your brain needs a steady flow of energy. Where does it get it? From the foods you eat.

Today, many factors contribute to a healthy diet, far more than merely balancing the five basic food groups. Eating "close to the earth," drinking plenty of pure water, controlling our fat, sugar, and salt intake, and limiting our ingestion of preservatives, additives, and chemically-treated foods are critical elements for optimal brain and body efficiency. Beyond this, a healthy diet requires sufficient protein, carbohydrate, good fats, fiber for bulk, and adequate vitamin and mineral intake. A diet that includes plenty of fresh fruits, vegetables, whole grains, and a protein source may supply the necessary carbohydrates, B vitamins, antioxidants, and essential amino acids required of your brain; however, the more we learn about nutrition and our bodies, the more factors we realize are at play. The purpose of this section is to provide a general framework for good memory health. In it we'll focus on the dietary elements that directly impact your cognitive functioning. It is not meant to be prescriptive in nature; and as in all matters related to your individual health, the advice of a healthcare professional should be sought if you are experiencing problems or want to modify your current lifestyle. "Suggestions for Further Study" are included in the appendix.

■ *Feeding the Hungry Brain*

Simply put and straight to the point, your mental fitness is highly dependent upon how well you eat. Why? Because the NEUROTRANSMITTERS that are responsible for all cell communication throughout your body are directly influenced by what you consume. To carry out this important work, the brain requires vast amounts of energy—more, in fact, than any other organ in your body. Despite the fact that your brain makes up only 2 percent

The brain is by far the "hungriest" organ in the body. It consumes eight to ten times more glucose and oxygen than other organs, pound for pound, though it represents only 2 percent of total body weight.

of your total body weight, it uses almost 20 percent of your body's oxygen intake. Whether you're sleeping, reading, or running a marathon, your brain requires a constant supply of fuel derived from oxygen and glucose (blood-sugar) fed to it through your bloodstream. If you do not receive the nutrition you need to make energy, your brain is the first to suffer. This is true because, unlike your liver and muscles, which store energy for later retrieval, the brain has no energy storage capacity. If the glucose level in your blood drops low enough, your brain will draw it away from other organs. When this happens, at best, you will become foggy-headed and find it difficult to concentrate. At worst, symptoms such as aggressive or irritable feelings, loss of self-control, blurred vision, amnesia, and a reduction in thinking and reasoning ability—known collectively as hypoglycemia—are the result. It is within your power, however, to eliminate this common experience; and all you have to do is maintain an adequate supply of energy to your brain. Before we explore further the impact of diet on memory, consider the following questions. Don't worry about answering them "correctly." The purpose of the inquiry is to get you *thinking about* (as opposed to judging harshly) your own dietary experiences and patterns; because, as you know, we are more likely to remember information that holds personal meaning for us and relates to our own life.

Memory Booster
Noticing Your Brain's Diet

Take a few moments to answer the following questions in your Memory Journal. The questions are designed to increase your awareness of your eating habits, not to assess your diet. Your answers will, of course, be more general than real life warrants; don't worry about that. Rather answer the questions in relation to the past month or week, looking for mere patterns and generalities, rather than concentrating on the exceptions and uncertainties that exist in all of our lives. Once you've focused on your own diet, the information in this chapter will have more relevance and meaning; thus, it will be better integrated into your memory system.

- **What foods would a typical breakfast for you consist of; and in what order would you most likely eat them?**

- **What foods would a typical lunch for you consist of; and in what order would you likely eat them?**

- **What foods would a typical dinner for you consist of; and in what order would you likely eat them?**

- **Do you eat candy and other sugary foods or drink sweet beverages? How often and how much? How do you feel afterwards?**

- **Do you consume diet foods/beverages? How many and what sugar substitute do they contain?**

- **How do you know that you're getting sufficient nutrition? Or do you?**

- **Do you often skip meals? If so, is it usually the same one(s)?**

- **Do you sometimes find yourself getting suddenly irritable with people?**

- **Do you take any dietary supplements regularly? What nutrients do they contain?**

- **How often do you snack? What foods do you typically snack on?**

- **Do you drink coffee or caffeinated beverages? If so, how many cups or cans per day?**

- **How often do you eat fast foods, packaged meals, or other highly-processed foods?**

- **How much water do you drink each day?**

- **Do you drink alcoholic beverages? If so, how many?**

- **Do you purchase organic products when possible?**

- **Do you often feel mentally sluggish?**

- **Do you take any nutritional supplements? If so, which ones?**

When you're finished reading this chapter, reconsider the dietary habits you've adopted. Are there any changes you might wish to make? Record your thoughts in your Memory Journal.

■ Smart Foods and Wise Choices

Walking into a health food store the size of a Sears can be an overwhelming experience—intimidating at worst and a virtual circus for our senses at best. It also highlights the wealth of choices available nowadays for feeding our hungry brains. Unfortunately, many factors contribute to poor dietary decisions—conflicting opinions and studies, commercially motivated fads, competing demands on our attention and resources, and a bombardment of messages on the subconscious. The study of nutrition as it relates to memory is dynamic and still young. It includes the effects of vitamins, minerals, amino acids, and "brain enhancing" supplements. Here's a synthesis.

Good nutrition promotes healthy functioning of neurons—the essential building blocks of mental performance.

■ Protein Power

Protein is required to keep the "chemical soup" of NEUROTRANSMITTERS in your brain functioning at optimal levels. Though protein is not readily converted to glucose for immediate energy, it is broken down by digestion into molecules of amino acids, which are the building blocks of neurotransmitters. This does not mean you need to eat great amounts of protein or that protein will make you any smarter, but going without it will reduce your mental functions.

If you need to be at peak mental efficiency following a meal, you have a couple of choices. You can eat a protein-only meal, consisting preferably of low-fat items like fish, poultry, or lean meat. Or the more preferable option is to eat a meal that provides a lean protein, a little fat, some carbohydrate, and an overall moderate amount of calories. Many nutritionists recommend that if your meal mixes proteins and carbohydrates, eat at least one-third of the protein source first before consuming anything else. In short, if the carbohydrate source reaches your brain before the protein source does, a sluggish response may occur. Here's why.

■ The Amino Acid Brain Race

Two important amino acids—tryptophan (derived from carbohydrates) and tyrosine (derived from proteins)—are in competition with each other to get to your brain first after you eat. If you plan to relax or go to sleep after you eat, you want tryptophan to win; but if you want to be mentally alert, you want tyrosine to win. Here's a silly MNEMONIC to help you remember which is which:

The ski racers took their place. *Carbo,* known as *"Spaghetti-Head,"* went first. When he *tripped* at the gate, however, he decided to *sit out* a race. *Pro-Teen*, known as *"Meat-Head,"* on the other hand, made a good start, *finished first*, and *"tied* one on" as the *brainy* winner.

The reason why tryptophan causes sluggishness is because it stimulates the neurotransmitter SEROTONIN, while tyrosine stimulates the neurotransmitters DOPAMINE, NOREPINEPHRINE, and EPINEPHRINE. How might you create an association to remember these additional facts?

Case Study
Food for Thought

In a study conducted at the Massachusetts Institute of Technology, researchers gave forty men (18 to 28 years old) a turkey lunch (3 ounces of protein). Afterwards, they asked them to do some complicated mental tasks. On another day, they provided the men with a four-ounce lunch of wheat starch—almost

pure carbohydrate—and challenged their mental powers in an equivalent manner. Not surprising to nutritionists, the subjects showed a significant reduction in mental performance after the carbohydrate lunch when compared to the earlier protein lunch. Other studies have duplicated the findings and further suggest that adults over forty-years-old are even more likely than those younger to experience the carbohydrate effect. In fact, the older set had up to twice the difficulty concentrating, remembering, and performing mental tasks after a high-carbohydrate lunch than those in the same age group who had eaten a pure protein meal.

■ *Calming Carbohydrates*

The good news about the concentration-enhancing power of protein does not mean that carbohydrates should be scratched from the race. There's a place at the table for bread, pasta, potatoes, and sherbet too. And that place is when you want to chill out, unwind, and de-stress. The mood mechanisms in your brain are so sensitive, that even a small amount of a particular food type can have an immediate and noticeable effect on your mind and body. Just an ounce or two, for example, of carbohydrates (a sweet or starchy food) is sufficient to reduce stress and calm your nerves, according to Dr. Judith Wurtman, author of *Managing Your Mind & Mood Through Food*.

One study conducted by Temple University Medical School and Texas Tech University found that, in fact, the drowsiness level of women (18 to 29 years old) doubled when they ate a high-carbohydrate lunch. The obvious tip is this: For the Valentine's Day breakfast-in-bed, go ahead and pile on the biscuits, butter, and jam. However, for that high-powered lunch where your mental clarity may mean the difference between a promotion or not, the grilled fish dish or chicken salad is the better choice.

Brain Workout
Pig Out and Put On Your Thinking Cap

Are you ready to test your own concentration after eating a "power lunch"? You can set up a simple experiment by comparing your cognitive performance on the following exercises after first eating a high-carbohydrate meal, and then on another day (a week or so later) after eating a protein-rich meal where at least one-third of the protein source is consumed before anything else. Record the results of your experiment in your Memory Journal. Exercise 2 and Part II of Exercise 1 continue on page 124.

Exercise 1 (part I)

One-half-hour after eating a carbohydrate-rich meal, do the following exercise, as well as Exercise 2 on page 124. Write down your results. The second time you will eat a protein-rich meal prior to the exercises. Are you ready? Okay, study the ten shapes at left for one minute. Try to commit them to memory. Then turn to page 124 and follow the directions first for Exercise 2 and then Exercise 1, part II.

Good Fats, Bad Fats

Have you been following the fat facts of life for awhile? If so, perhaps you've already joined the stream of converts who have successfully made the transition from the love of real butter to the heart-loving choice of soybean or olive oil. Not only is this choice better for your body, it is better for your brain. Here's one of the landmark studies in support of your healthy choice.

In studying the effects of dietary fat on learning, Dr. Carol Greenwood, Associate Professor of Nutrition at the University of Toronto, and colleagues compared three groups of animals fed three different diets: Group One's diet was rich in polyunsaturated fats from soybean oil; Group Two's diet was high in saturated fats from lard; and Group Three received their standard fare to provide a baseline comparison. The researchers tested the animals' ability to learn twenty-one days after their diets began and found that not only did the animals who received the soybean oil learn about 20 percent faster than the other two groups, they were less likely to forget what they learned.

Fat is a necessary element in our diet. In fact, it provides much of the raw material from which our brain cells are made. The key, however, is moderate consumption of good fat, such as that which is found in safflower, sunflower, olive, or soybean oils, and in foods such as avocados, nuts, and fish. Metabolizing fat is a laborious process for the body; it takes much longer than other nutrients. To accomplish the task blood is diverted from other organs to the stomach. Consequently, blood flow is reduced in the brain, which explains why a drop in concentration occurs after a high-fat meal. A high-fat diet (more than 30% of total dietary calories) contributes to the development of fatal diseases such as heart disease, stroke, and cancer; and it has been shown to slow thinking processes. A low-fat diet will make digestion easier, keep your arteries healthy, and will support greater mental clarity and concentration—a precursor to good memory. Now, you decide which is the better choice.

The Caffeine Question

What's your take on coffee? Do you drink it? Do you drink other caffeinated beverages? How much? Do you wish you didn't? The coffee court's been out on the question of caffeine's effects for many years. It seems that this favorite international pastime reflects one of the many common dietary contradictions. In one study at the University of North Carolina at Charlotte, researchers discovered that the amount of caffeine in a single cup of coffee can reduce your recall of newly learned material; and yet, another study conducted at Massachusetts Institute of Technology, found that caffeine improved the mental performance of subjects on various mental measurements (Wurtman 1988). In spite of the contradictory nature of these reports, there is little scientific evidence that caffeine has any harmful long-term effects on health when taken in

moderation. "For every report indicating a link between caffeine and a major health problem, another study done by equally respected and disinterested investigators, indicates little or no such connection," says Dr. Judith Wurtman.

The coffee paradox is that while it's certainly a brain stimulant, it decreases blood flow to your brain at the same time. This is why caffeine is used in the treatment of migraine headaches; it helps to contract the distended blood vessels in the brain. There's no question that a caffeinated beverage provides a quick mental lift that can last for up to six hours. However, the popular cliché, moderation is best, applies here. Caffeine can have adverse side effects on some individuals. If you are an insomniac, or get jittery or sweaty, or experience headaches or stomach upset when you consume caffeinated beverages then, of course, you should stop. You might consider replacing your morning cup of Java with a can of Smartz™ or another mental fitness drink. Look for those that contain phosphatidyl choline, phosphatidylserine, and a host of other memory-enhancing nutrients. These tasty supplements will have a similar effect on your brain as coffee, but without the high caffeine content.

While caffeine is certainly a brain stimulant, it also decreases blood flow to your brain; thus, moderation is important.

■ *The Sugar Question*

The chemical energy that fuels your brain's communication and protein manufacturing processes is derived almost exclusively from glucose (a simple sugar). Research conducted in Great Britain studied the effects of a high glucose drink given to school children in the late afternoon. Their concentration improved markedly and they showed less frustration when asked to perform difficult tasks. Does this mean we should feed children a sugar snack in conjunction with learning? Probably not, say most nutritionists, because many children (and adults) eat far too much sugar. In fact, in some cases a high-sugar diet has been linked to hyperactivity disorders and learning disabilities in children. The fact remains, however, that our bodies depend on blood sugar (glucose) for energy. It is not a good idea, therefore, to try and learn something or tend to an important matter in a state of low blood sugar. Recent evidence suggests that starches may produce a faster rise in blood sugar levels than sugar. With this in mind, the recommended brain snack is some crackers or cookies. Despite the notion that fruit will give you this added energy effect, fructose (sugar from fruit) does not provide your brain directly with energy because fructose cannot pass the BLOOD BRAIN BARRIER. Table sugar (a combination of glucose and fructose), however can (Chaftez 1992; Gold 1995).

■ *The Supplement Debate: Why or Why Not?*

Do you believe in taking nutritional supplements? This question invariably generates a lively discussion. People on one side of the debate believe that if you include a variety of whole foods and fresh fruits and vegetables in your diet, your vitamin levels should be adequate. Others, however, contend that since the body does not store water-soluble vitamins, and many of us eat what's convenient in a pinch rather than what's nutritional, and some nutrients are difficult to obtain in adequate amounts from foods we eat, a supplement ensures good nutrition.

Figure 6.1

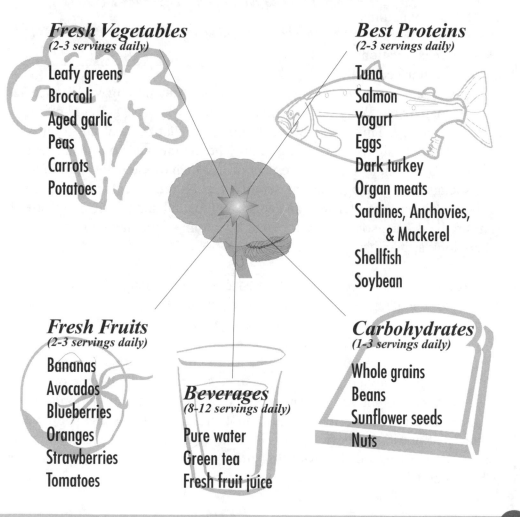

Brain Food Recommendations

Fresh Vegetables
(2-3 servings daily)

Leafy greens
Broccoli
Aged garlic
Peas
Carrots
Potatoes

Best Proteins
(2-3 servings daily)

Tuna
Salmon
Yogurt
Eggs
Dark turkey
Organ meats
Sardines, Anchovies,
    & Mackerel
Shellfish
Soybean

Fresh Fruits
(2-3 servings daily)

Bananas
Avocados
Blueberries
Oranges
Strawberries
Tomatoes

Beverages
(8-12 servings daily)

Pure water
Green tea
Fresh fruit juice

Carbohydrates
(1-3 servings daily)

Whole grains
Beans
Sunflower seeds
Nuts

In a perfect world nutritional supplements would not be necessary. We would all eat close to the earth—that is, unprocessed organic natural foods without preservatives and environmental pollutants. However, as the American diet has become widely reliant on highly-processed fast foods and as our environments have been exposed to toxins of many kinds, the average person's nutrition has suffered immeasurably. Enriching your diet with herbs, nutritional supplements, and in some cases, synthetic-chemical compounds, may be necessary for you to receive optimal nutrition. Many people report an increase in mental energy and concentration as a result of nutritional supplementation. They also find that this level of alertness can be sustained over longer periods of time with less sleep. These attributes, which are the backbone of learning, are highly desired for keeping up with the pace of our world today.

Of course, the correction of a problem is always more noticeable than its prevention since there are fewer symptoms to serve as a basis for judging rehabilitation in the latter case.

Proper nutrition helps protect the brain against damage from environmental toxins and ensures we receive adequate supplies of oxygen essential for maintaining a high energy level.

Thus, people who are closer to optimal mental functioning will notice less improvement upon taking supplements than those who have suffered more pronounced damage. This does not mean, however, that optimal nutrition is not important to the highly functioning brain. The maintenance of mental strength is just as important as the improvement of it. Much of the deterioration usually associated with aging, such as senility, can be reduced, for example, with proper nutritional maintenance and consistent mental and physical exercise. To sum up the debate, some people look at a vitamin supplement and say "why"; others look at it and say "why not"?

The key here is to become an educated consumer. Many physicians refrain from recommending supplements to their patients because in extreme doses, some vitamins are toxic and can interact negatively with prescribed drugs, such as heart medications. On the other hand, many people can clearly benefit from supplements taken responsibly. One factor to consider is that it is not always easy to recognize a vitamin deficiency since symptoms like fatigue or a weakened immune system can be caused by a variety of conditions, only one of which is a nutritional deficiency. Still another issue is that some people don't realize that nutritional deficiencies do, indeed, impact their cognitive performance in addition to their physical health. Are you feeling mentally sluggish? Why not consider all the possibilities?

Even mild malnutrition or other dietary imbalances can make it harder for children and adults to learn. A 1988 study of Welsh schoolchildren concluded that taking a vitamin and mineral supplement increased their non-verbal intelligence scores—a finding that suggests their pre-study diets to begin with were deficient in the range of vitamins and minerals necessary for optimal mental performance. In addition, a

Usually the first indication of a nutritional deficiency is a decline in mental functioning.

British study of ninety twelve to thirteen-year-olds came to the same conclusion. And a study of adults conducted by the University of New Mexico School of Medicine reported a correlation between low blood levels of vitamins C, B-12, riboflavin, and folic acid and lower scores on standard tests for memory and nonverbal abstract-thinking ability.

These studies underscore the importance of staying up with current findings in the nutrition field. Scientists have determined that there are forty-five *essential* nutrients—that is, nutrients that are absolutely necessary for good health and that cannot be made by your body unless you provide the proper building blocks through your diet. A lack of any essential nutrient will eventually result in a deterioration of health or a loss of brain function. These essential nutrients consist of

If it is the right of every child to receive an education, it must also be their right to receive the nutrition necessary to think. Thinking requires energy; energy requires proper nutrition.

twenty minerals, fifteen vitamins, eight essential amino acids, and two essential fatty acids. For optimal health, we need a sufficient amount of each of these elements. Although the RDA (Recommended Daily Allowance) provides a basic guideline for the quantities we need, RDAs were established many years ago and were based on *reducing* disease, rather than on *maintaining* optimum brain and body wellness.

■ *Brain-Building Vitamins and Minerals*

Vitamins play a key role in brain metabolism. Many studies have shown that vitamin deficiency is a common problem among the mentally ill and elderly. Even minor vitamin deficiencies can cause depression and mood disorders.

Vitamin A has very recently been found to play a role in learning and memory by researchers at the Salk Institute of Biological Studies in San Diego. "We have long known that vitamin A is an important ANTIOXIDANT and that it is needed for proper development of the nervous system in a growing embryo," reports Dr. Ronald Evans, senior author of the study. "This is the first evidence, however, that vitamin A is needed for brain function during life." Vitamin A exerts its effects by docking to various receptors on cells and triggering biochemical responses within the cell—a vital aspect of LONG-TERM POTENTIATION.

B vitamins, in particular, when not adequately consumed may contribute to depression, intellectual impairment, and even psychosis. B vitamins are important in mental functioning because they are the catalysts, without which many chemical reactions in the brain cannot take place. A diet lacking vitamin B complex, especially B-1, B-3, and B-12, can produce memory impairment. Anything that depletes B-1 (thiamine), such as stress, alcohol, drugs, or poor nutrition can result in short-term memory loss and other cognitive functions. A deficiency in B-3 (niacin) can lead to nervousness, insomnia, irritability, depression, anxiety, and confusion. And a deficiency in B-12 (cyanocobalamin) can lead to trouble focusing and remembering, depression, and even hallucinations. A simple B-complex supplement, however, can ensure your brain has enough B vitamins to convert proteins and carbohydrates in your diet into vital mental energy.

Vitamin C helps your brain use protein to make the NEUROTRANSMITTERS that are integral to thinking and remembering. A University of New Mexico Medical School study found that when they compared blood levels of vitamin C in subjects, the lower the C, the lower their scores were on tests measuring short-term memory and problem-solving skills. Vitamin C is also an important ANTIOXIDANT.

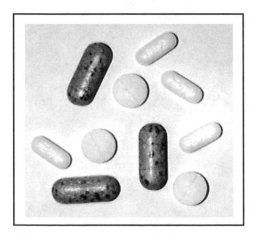

Even minor vitamin deficiencies can cause depression, mood disorders, and short-term memory loss.

Vitamin E is essential in supplying oxygen to your muscles and protecting the healthy brain from the damaging effects of free radicals and the aging process. Preliminary studies suggest it may help slow the progression of Alzheimer's disease; The National Institute on Aging in Bethesda, Maryland recently announced that they are funding a twenty-two million dollar study spread across sixty-five centers in the United States to see whether a high dose vitamin E pill (selegeline) can prevent people who are just starting to have memory problems from progressing to dementia.

Although the study of minerals in brain wellness is relatively young, scientists have determined that three minerals in particular are especially imperative for good memory function—*boron*, *zinc*, and *magnesium*. In addition, *manganese*, *iron*, *calcium*, *copper*, and *selenium* have been shown to impact learning in some cases. Researchers at the USDA Human Nutrition Research Center found that three milligrams of *boron* a day improved people's alertness and learning ability. Dr. James Penland, a research scientist for the United States Department of Agriculture's Grand Forks Human Nutrition Research Center also found that less than adequate intakes of *boron*, *copper*, and *manganese* impair memory, thinking, and mood. Lack of *magnesium* can cloud your memory by retarding blood

> *Nutrition can readily boost the memory and mind by correcting abnormalities in the chemical environment of the brain.*
>
> —Linus Pauling

circulation in the brain; and a *zinc* deficiency, particularly in the elderly, has long been linked to mental confusion and even Alzheimer's disease. Women in studies conducted at the University of Texas discovered that their ability to remember words and visual patterns improved with *zinc* supplements; and a study conducted by Dr. Don Tucker of the University of Oregon found adults could improve alertness, memory, and even word fluency with an *iron* supplement. Children deficient in *iron* have been shown to have short attention spans and more trouble learning new material.

Nature's Bounty of Neuro-Nutrients

Individual differences in age, diet, health, nutrition status, biochemical variance, and interaction with other therapeutic agents makes providing a generic recommendation for neural-enhancement dosages problematic. Always consult a trusted nutrition professional or physician experienced in "alternative" therapies before starting a new supplement. Because of the dynamic nature of the field, we recommend that you use the following synopsis as a springboard for further study. For timely updates, see "Suggestions for Further Study" in the Appendix.

■ Amino Acids: Brain Sustenance

A total of twenty amino acids make up all the proteins found in the human body; twelve can be made within the body and are known as *nonessential*. The other eight, *essential* amino acids, must be obtained from the diet (or nutritional supplements). Scientists have found that supplements containing certain amino acids improve alertness, lessen fatigue, and boost mental agility. They hasten to point out, however, that taking large doses of any amino acid may eventually disrupt the body's metabolic balance. Thus, moderation, once again. is recommended.

Phenylalanine

Phenylalanine is an essential amino acid that supplies the raw material for the manufacture of catecholamines—a class of NEUROTRANSMITTERS that includes NOREPINEPH-RINE, EPINEPHRINE, and DOPAMINE. Catecholamines, known as the alertness and ambition enhancers, are essential in the transmission of nerve impulses. Phenylalanine has been shown to reverse depression (over 80 percent of the time), improve attention span, learning, and memory, and help control appetite. After ingesting phenylalanine, which occurs naturally in chicken, beef, fish, eggs, and soybeans, your body produces more tyrosine (important for alertness), dopa and dopamine (important in Parkinson's disease), and norepinephrine and epinephrine (important in learning and memory). An enzyme that reduces norepinephrine in the body increases after the age of forty-five, so it is especially important to be aware of phenylalanine and its effects as you age.

Tyrosine

Another amino acid called tyrosine (see also p. 105) has been shown in clinical findings to be helpful in overcoming depression, improving memory, and increasing mental alertness. Contained naturally in chicken liver, cheese, avocado, bananas, yeast, fish, and meat, tyrosine was declared by the U.S. Army Research Institute of Environmental Medicine at Natick, Massachusetts in 1988 as superior to both stimulant drugs and tranquilizers for enhancing mental and physical performance under stress, without side effects. The body can make tyrosine from left-over phenylalanine—another amino acid—and they both produce the neurotransmitter norepinephrine, which influences mood and impacts learning. Most memory supplements include in their active ingredients phenylalanine, tyrosine, and glutamine.

Glutamine

A nonessential amino acid called glutamic acid acts as a brain fuel and controls excess ammonia, which forms in the body as a result of bio-chemical processes. The most interesting thing about glutamic acid, however, is that besides glucose, it is the only other compound that serves as fuel for your brain. Naturally, glutamic acid is found in whole wheat and soybeans. In the past, the problem with enhancing the levels of glutamic acid for better recall and learning has been its inability to be absorbed by the brain in supplemental form. The good news is, however, that researchers have discovered a form of glutamic acid, glutamine, which does cross through the protective barrier of the brain to enhance intelligence. Beyond its benefit to memory, glutamine has been shown to speed the healing of ulcers, and to have positive effects in controlling alcoholism, schizophrenia, fatigue, and the craving for sweets.

It's not hard to imagine serious brain athletes getting their gray matter in shape by pumping peptides and neurotransmitters.

—Michael Hutchison
Megabrain

◼ *Phospholipids: Lubricating Your Brain Cells*

Phospholipids are naturally occurring brain-cell fats; and include phosphatidyl choline, phosphatidyl serine, phosphatidyl ethanolamine, and phosphatidyl inositol. All of the phospholipids promote membrane fluidity which is crucial for cellular responsiveness, nutrient processing, and information transfer. Phosphatidyl choline and phosphatidyl serine, however, have been implicated as possible aids to memory by respectively increasing the amount of acetylcholine in the brain, and by activating brain metabolism and cell fluidity.

Phosphatidyl Choline

The dietary substance choline is the forerunner of the NEUROTRANSMITTER, ACETYLCHOLINE, important in learning and memory. Choline has been experimentally demonstrated in humans to improve memory, thinking ability, muscle control, and serial-type learning in some studies. Dr. Christian Gillin, government scientist and top official at the National Institute of Health, reports "Our tests show that giving people choline increases their memory and learning ability by a startling 25 percent." The production of acetylcholine, which is vital for the transmission of messages from one nerve cell to another, is increased as choline is consumed. According to government scientists, it is these "thought wave paths" that are believed to be responsible for the memory process.

Choline can be obtained from lecithin-rich foods such as egg yolks, salmon, wheat, soybeans, and lean beef. A concentrated form of choline called phosphatidyl choline (PC) can be taken in simple pill form and is available at most health food stores. Lecithin concentrates provide a natural source of PC, however, phosphatidyl inositol and phosphatidyl ethanolamine, which are also contained in lecithin, compete for

There is more than a bone *of truth in the old adage that fish is "brain food." In general, fish contains more natural cognitive enhancers than any other food known.*

absorption with PC in this form. The most effective way to absorb PC, therefore, may be the 75 percent pure form, such as Phos Chol 900, which is free of other phosphatides. Phos Chol 900 is available under a variety of brand names. No side effects are known and studies indicate a 50 percent increase in choline levels when supplementing with three capsules per day.

Phosphatidyl Serine

According to Dr. Thomas Crook, a clinical psychologist and researcher at the Memory Assessment Clinics of Bethesda, Maryland, a supplement of phosphatidyl serine (PS), a naturally occurring fatty acid in the brain, may reverse up to twelve years of age-related mental decline. In his studies, patients given 100 to 300 mg. of PS daily showed a 15 percent improvement in learning ability and other memory tasks (Crook 1998). Human trials dating back to the 1970s support Crook's findings. In addition to aiding AGE-ASSOCIATED MENTAL DECLINE, PS benefits may be seen in patients with Parkinson's disease, Alzheimer's disease, epilepsy, and the depression that is associated with mental decline in the elderly. PS works by activating metabolism in almost all regions of the brain, as seen in PET scans and on EEGs. PS has also been shown to restore flexibility to the membranes in the cell structure when stiffened by the aging process.

■ Other Memory/Mind Essentials

Ribonucleic Acid

Ribonucleic Acid (RNA) and deoxyribonucleic acid (DNA) exist in the nucleus of every cell: They carry our genetic code, and direct the production of proteins. RNA is a key piece in the learning and memory puzzle. In startling studies conducted in the 1970s, RNA transplanted from  one group of trained mice to another resulted in the transfer of the learned behaviors, as well. In other studies animals given RNA supplements learned quickly and experienced a 20 percent longer lifespan. When injected, however, with an enzyme that destroys RNA, they were unable to learn. In humans, RNA is an important factor in tissue repair, healing, and brain development; and is found naturally in fish (especially sardines), shellfish, onions, and brewers yeast. Supplements claim to enhance brain power and memory and protect against damage caused by oxidation of fats.

NADH

In clinical trials, 80 percent of Parkinson's patients experienced benefits from NADH (Nicotinamide Adenine Dinucleotide) supplements. A relative newcomer to the field of nutrition and natural healing, NADH supplements have been shown to, among other benefits, increase brain activity and motor ability in patients suffering from Alzheimer's, Parkinson's, chronic fatigue, and depression. Increased concentration, energy, mood, and stamina are reported in healthy subjects, as well (Birkmayer 1996). Biologically known as Coenzyme 1, NADH is present in all living cells and plays a central role in the body's energy producing capacity, particularly in the brain and central nervous system. It works by stimulating the production of DOPAMINE and other NEUROTRANSMITTERS.

Estrogen

The hormone estrogen has been found to support brain function and is being used in the treatment today of Alzheimer's patients. Dr. Barbara Sherwin, co-director of the McGill University Menopause Clinic, revealed estrogen's importance by testing verbal memory in young women before and after they underwent treatment for uterine tumors. The women's estrogen levels fell dramatically after chemotherapy treatments, as did their scores on reading-retention tests. However, when half of the women were given estrogen replacement, their performance promptly rebounded. Estrogen appears to work by stimulating SYNAPSE growth, output of ACETYLCHOLINE, and the flow of blood in the brain, which provides more oxygen and glucose. The downside of estrogen therapy for memory enhancement is that some studies report a possible increased risk of breast cancer. A 1998 observational study of 700-plus healthy post-menopausal women, led by researchers from Columbia University College of Physicians and Surgeons, found that those who used estrogen replacement therapy scored significantly higher than non-users on memory tests as well as performing better on language and abstract reasoning tests.

Ginkgo Biloba

The oldest living tree known to humans has been shown to enhance memory functioning in healthy adults and to restore memory functioning in patients with chronic cerebral insufficiency. Administered orally in extract form, the Ginkgo herb significantly improves circulation. Improved circulation means more nutrients and oxygen are delivered to the brain, resulting in improved brain function. In studies with both healthy subjects and subjects with chronic cere-bral insufficiency, results showed significant

improvement in short-term memory. Reports also claim that ginkgo extracts increase the supply and utilization of glucose, which is the brain's primary source of fuel and energy. Research has shown that a Ginkgo extract which is standardized to provide a complex mixture of 24 percent flavonglycosides is most effective. The flavonglycosides should include those that give Ginkgo its active properties: ginkgolide A, ginkgolide B, ginkgolide C, and bilobalides.

DHA

Recent studies suggest that DHA (Docosahexaenoic Acid), the primary structural fatty acid in our brain's gray matter, is important to mental performance at every stage of our life. DHA, a form of omega-3 essential fatty acid, is a natural anti-inflammatory agent that protects cell membranes against oxidative damage and increas-

es cellular fluidity. In addition, it may aid depression and those suffering from Alzheimer's. In 1993, both the Food and Agricultural Organization and the World Health Organization acknowledged DHA's importance in brain development when studies reported a link between lower concentration of omega-3 fatty acids in infant formulas (versus breast milk) with lower intelligence in children who consumed formula. As a result of these findings, DHA is now being added to some infant formulas. Adult studies have reported that eating one serving or more of fish per week reduced the risk of getting Alzheimer's by 70 percent compared to non-fish eaters. Researchers postulate that this protection effect is linked to the anti-inflammatory activity of the omega-3 fatty acids in fish oil. Omega -3 is also found in flax and hemp oil; and natural supplements of either omega-3 or DHA (alone) are available. Although it is important to balance omega-3 and omega-6 essential fatty acids in your diet, most Americans get way too much omega-6 fats and are seriously deficient in omega-3 fats.

Acetyl-l-carnitine

Acetyl-l-carnitine (ALC), closely related to the amino acid carnitine, is a natural compound that improves energy exchange between cells and strengthens intercellular communication between the brain's right and left hemispheres. More than fifty human trials have been done with ALC since 1990. ALC is currently being tested in clinical trials as a cognitive enhancer for Alzheimer's patients. A study of five-hundred geriatric patients supports the finding that older people showing signs of mental decline experienced noticeably sharpened thinking skills after taking an ALC supplement. The patients who received ALC (rather than the placebo) showed "significant increases" in scores of mental function tests; while those who were given the placebo showed no significant improvement. Italian researchers published a landmark study in 1992, which suggests that ALC improves mental performance in young, healthy people (Lino et al. 1992); and Romanian studies with elite athletes suggest l-carnitine improves the biological potential of the body (Dragan, Wagner, Ploesteanu 1988).

DHEA

DHEA (Dehydroepiandrosterone), known as the "mother of hormones" because it gets converted into dozens of other hormones by the body, is a neurosteroid produced by the adrenal glands. Although our body produces plentiful quantities of it in our twenties, by age sixty-five, our DHEA production drops dramatically. In mostly animal studies, DHEA has been shown to enhance memory (particularly long-term memory) and learning. In rats DHEA stimulates the production of a key brain cell messenger and the growth of SYNAPSES that carry signals between cells. Human studies suggest DHEA supplements may normalize potentially dangerous affects of high CORTISOL levels from excessive stress. Some doctors hesitate to recommend DHEA because of the uncertainty over long-term side effects. The right dosage of DHEA is important, so you should consult a physician and have your hormone levels tested before starting it.

Pregnenolone

A precursor of DHEA, pregnenolone, is also on the fast-track in memory studies. Pregnenolone, used for decades for treating arthritis, is completely non-toxic and exhibits no side-effects. Although it has been proven to increase speed and quality of learning in mice, pregnenolone is still in trials with patients who have mild to severe Alzheimer's disease, as well as with healthy older people with AGE-ASSOCIATED MEMORY IMPAIRMENT (AAMI) or MILD COGNITIVE IMPAIRMENT (MCI).

Piracetam

Probably the most widely known and used cognitive enhancer, Piracetam has been described as the smart drug of the decade for normal, healthy people. Both animal and human studies conducted over the past two decades confirm that Piracetam enhances learning and memory. The following broad effects are reported: reduces metabolic stress in low-oxygen conditions; increases rate of metabolism and neuronal energy; is effective with both healthy and memory-impaired individuals; slows down AAMI; is not selective
(works in most cases); and facilitates cellular communication between left and right hemispheres of the brain. The potential clinical applications for Piracetam are numerous—from treating Alzheimer's and epilepsy to attention deficit disorder and dyslexia. Piracetam has no known contraindications; it is

safe and without toxicity. Although it is not yet marketed in the United States, it is available in other countries under various trade names, such as Nootropyl™ and Nootropil™.

Nimodipine

Nimodipine, a calcium-channel blocker (usually prescribed for heart conditions), has been described as remarkable for its breadth of effects. In addition to holding much promise in the treatment of Alzheimer's disease, nimodipine is being tested for its effectiveness in improving AAMI. Nimodipinine increases blood flow in the brain by preventing constriction of cerebral blood vessels. Although, FDA approved since 1989 for treatment of hemorrhagic stroke, nimodipine appears to have a wider therapeutic usefulness. In clinical trials with elderly people showing some AAMI, researchers have reported a protective effect in stress-related illnesses; improved memory, depression, and general state of mind; and anxiety reduction. Rare adverse side effects have been reported. The drug should not be used in conjunction with other calcium-channel blockers, nor without consulting your physician. Trade names for this prescription medication include Nimotop™ and Periplum™.

DMAE

DMAE (dimethylaminoethanol), known generically as deanol or by its trade name Deaner™, is a well-known , safe, and natural brain stimulant that appears to optimize production of ACETYLCHOLINE, the primary NEUROTRANS-MITTER involved in learning and memory. Results from early clinical trials reported DMAE was especially effective with patients suffering from chronic fatigue and mild to moderate depression. Since that time, DMAE has also been reported to stimulate lucid dreaming, improve memory and learning, increase intelligence, and extend life span. DMAE was FDA approved in 1983 for treating learning disorders in children; however, the production was later discontinued due to stiffer governmental requirements coupled with profitability issues. DMAE, a precursor to choline and a naturally occurring nutrient in anchovies and sardines, can directly cross the BLOOD-BRAIN BARRIER, while choline cannot. It produces a mild stimulation without a drug-like letdown or depression when discontinued.

More than one hundred NOOTROPICS or "brain agents" are currently under development worldwide—particularly for the treatment of Alzheimer's, and AAMI or MCI. The dynamic nature of the field makes it impossible to provide an exhaustive list of all the products available. The aforementioned list, however, represents the most popularly used agents and the most current information available about them at the time of printing. A description of common prescription medications used for treating Alzheimer's—Ampalex™, Aricept™, Cognex™—and the herbal extract, Huperzine A, is included in Chapter 8.

Anti-Memory-Loss Supplements

Vitamins

Vitamin A
Vitamin B Complex
Vitamin C with Riboflavinoids
Vitamin E
Pyritynol (vitamin B-6)

Minerals

Magnesium
Zinc
Boron
Calcium
Selenium
Copper
Iron
Manganese

Drugs

Ampalex or CX-516 - (ampakine)
Aricept™ - (donepezil)
Cognex™ - (tacrine)
Estrogen

Products

Phenylalanine
Glutamine
Tyrosine
RNA- (ribonucleic acid)
NADH - (nicotinamide adenine dinucleotide)
Acetyl-l-carnitine
DHEA - (dehydroepiandrosterone)
Ginkgo Biloba
Phosphatydyl Serine
Piracetam - (Nootropyl™ & Nootropil™)
Nimodipine - (Nimotop™ & Periplum™)
Pregnenolone
Phosphatidyl Choline
DMAE (dimethylaminoethanol) also known as Deanol
Non-Steroidal Anti-Inflammatories
DHA (docosahexaenoic acid)
Hyperzine or Huperzine A (Hep A)

Beverages

Caffeine - (limit to moderation)
Cerebroplex - (mental-fitness capsules)
Smartz™ - (mental-fitness drink)

Individual differences in age, diet, health, nutrition status, biochemical variance, and interaction with other therapeutic agents makes generic dosage recommendations inaccurate in many cases. Always consult a trusted nutrition professional or physician experienced in "alternative" therapies before starting a new supplement. Many of these agents have not been FDA approved yet; and if not available at nutrition stores, may be obtained from overseas sources. We recommend that you use this synopsis of neural-enhancement supplements as a springboard for further study. More than one hundred NOOTROPIC agents are currently under investigation for their potential benefits to memory and cognitive functioning. See "Suggested Resources for Further Study" in the Appendix.

TOP-10 SUPER

1 **Fish:** *(Especially cold-water, i.e., trout, salmon, tuna, herring, mackerel and sardines)* lecithin (choline), phenylalanine, ribonucleic acid, tyrosine, DMAE, vitamin B-6, niacin/B-3, copper, good protein source, zinc, omega-3 fatty acids (DHA), vitamin B-12

2 **Eggs:**
phenylalanine, lecithin (choline), vitamin B-6, vitamin E

3 **Soybeans:**
lecithin (choline), glutamic acid, phenylalanine, vitamin E, iron, zinc, good protein source, vitamin B-6

4 **Lean Beef:**
phenylalanine, lecithin (choline), tyrosine, glutamic acid, iron, zinc

5 **Chicken Livers:**
tyrosine, vitamin A, vitamin B-1, vitamin B-6, vitamin B-12, good protein source, iron

MEMORY FOODS

6 ***Whole Wheat:***
lecithin (choline), glutamic acid, vitamin B-6, magnesium, vitamin E, vitamin B-1

7 ***Chicken:*** phenylalanine, vitamin B-6, niacin/B-3, good protein source

8 ***Bananas:***
tyrosine, magnesium, potassium, vitamin B-6

9 ***Low-Fat Dairy Products:***
phenylalanine, tyrosine, glutamine, good protein source, ALC, vitamin B-12

10 ***Avocados:***
tyrosine, magnesium

Exercise 2

The following simple exercise was developed by the Dutch Airforce to evaluate pilots' concentration skills. How would you like to test yours? Here's what you do. Set a timer for thirty seconds. Then count as many 4's and g's as you can find in the grid without taking any notes or marking on the page. When the buzzer sounds, write down your answers. Turn the book upside down for the answer key. When you do the exercise again (a week or more later) to compare your performance after a high-protein meal, identify the quantities of a different number and letter.

```
a 7 3 d g t p 9 6 2 x d e o
e w q d c 5 6 0 i d g v c d
w 3 6 7 9 w d z x j g e 2 3
7 b f d x c k l p o u t e e
4 c v b n m s w e r u i o p
h 4 f d s a q w s r t y u i
7 o e r t y u i 4 d e r g f
r t y u i c s w r d w 2 5 3
4 4 d 3 s w e d 3 5 h t c e
3 c d f g h y w s q x d 7 a
```

—continued from page 106

Exercise 1 (Part II)

On page 106 you were presented with ten shapes. Now, from memory, identify those figures. Included are distracting and similar shapes to make the exercise more challenging. Well, how did you do? Wait a week or so before doing the second half of the experiment (following a high-protein meal) so that you'll be starting fresh again.

Five 4's and three g's

*C*hapter Recollections

- Why is your brain so directly impacted by the foods you eat?

- What effect does a protein source have on your brain and learning?

- What effect does a carbohydrate source have on your brain and learning?

- What type of meal should you eat for a high-powered business luncheon?

- What is meant by good fats versus bad fats? What impact do each have on learning and memory?

- Which side of the caffeine debate do you find yourself on? How does caffeine personally impact you?

- Which side of the supplement debate are you on? Did you learn anything new about supplements in this chapter? What?

- What are some common symptoms of a vitamin and/or mineral deficiency? Why is it sometimes difficult to diagnose such a deficiency?

- What are some of the ways in which "nature's own nutrients" serve your memory?

Today's Lifestyle Effects on Memory

Chapter 7

Why Is Environment Important to Memory?

Once considered innate or fixed at conception, it is now recognized that memory skills are learned; and, thus, greatly impacted by environment. The implications of this finding are profound because it means if memory is mutable, it is improvable. Thus, this chapter focuses on the environmental factors that impact our memory on a day-to-day basis and the enrichment possibilities that are ever-inherent in our lifestyle choices.

It is probably no surprise to you that physical and mental health are interrelated; but did you realize that your physical health and memory are also linked. Even minor illness, such as a cold, or the flu, or undernourishment can have a mind-muddling effect. What specifically does this mean to the average person in this day and age? In the following pages, we will explore the ways in which stress, sleep, exercise, mood, drugs, alcohol, nicotine, and technology impact your memory, and what steps can be taken to achieve your highest memory potential. Never before has so much science backed the claim that our mental, physical, and emotional health are interdependent. Never before have we had such widespread understanding of and access to mental enrichment choices. Consider for a moment how your current lifestyle may be affecting your memory. Not sure? Keep reading.

*H*ow Does Stress Impact Memory?

Psychological stress is not inherently bad. In fact, life without any stress would be quite boring. There's little doubt that humankind's greatest achievements have been motivated, in part, as we've responded to some internal or external stressor. The anxiety, for example, usually associated with public speaking compels a speaker to practice their lines. Likewise, the fear of failing an exam motivates one to study. Project deadlines provide the impetus to get things done in an efficient manner, and the possibility of undesirable consequences helps offset danger and temper the wild beast in us. Even as we move through a normal day, all of our decisions and interactions are influenced by various conscious and unconscious stressors. This kind of moderate stress does not harm our memory, nor does dealing with a dangerous or life-threatening situation occasionally. The dangerous stress is more insidious than that—it is excessive and prolonged: It's the type that comes home from the office with you and doesn't go away at night. Here's how it works in the body.

The type of stress associated with daily fear or anxiety, major depression, or post-traumatic stress disorder inhibits memory and kills brain cells.

Good Stress, Bad Stress

The instant our hypothalamus senses danger it releases the chemical corticotrophin-releasing factor (CRF), while the pituitary releases ACTH. These two hormones directly influence the manufacture and release of stress hormones or GLUCOCORTICOIDS (including CORTISOL and ADRENALINE) resulting in an immediate alert response known as "fight or flight" mechanism or an adrenaline rush. When this happens, your sensory perception sharpens, your physical strength and energy elevate, time may slow down, and your memory is preserved—all automatic responses programmed in us to save our life. When cortisol is released in response to danger, our body uses it for survival, then dumps it. And when it is released in small amounts during the course of a normal day, our body uses it for increased arousal, motivation, action, and long-term memory.

When CORTISOL, however, is released in higher stress-induced concentrations over an extended period of time, it has an inhibiting effect on our memory and a toxic effect on NEURONS. Consequently, not only is your memory weakened, but your biological reaction to prolonged stress is the same as the biological result of aging (distress). To live with chronic stress, therefore, is to age prematurely. So although cortisol can be life-saving in moments of danger, it can cost brain cells over the long run, reports Dr. Robert Sapolsky of Stanford University, who reviewed recent studies of the long-term effects of the various stress hormones on the brain. His findings indicate that physical changes begin to occur in the HIPPOCAMPUS, a brain region important to learning and memory, in response to a major stressor or prolonged exposure to elevated cortisol levels from major depression, post-traumatic stress disorder, or a physiological malfunction. These physical changes may interfere with the ability to induce LONG-TERM POTENTIATION in the hippocampus: The result is memory failure (LeDoux 1996). The following figure illustrates the effects of stress levels on the body over time. And the "Stress Test" on the following page will help you assess your own stress level.

Figure 7.1

Stress, Trauma, and Memory

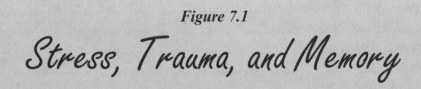

Stress Levels

Sustained Stress (Distress) or Trauma...
Results in impaired memory; memory becomes highly selective. Excess activation of cortisol from trauma or chronic stress commonly leads to neuronal death in the hippocampus.

Moderate Stress...
Results in general facilitation of memory storage; optimal hormonal activation.

Very Low Stress...
Results in neutral or minimal impact on memory; no excessive hormonal activation.

Memory Workout
Stress Test

The "Life-Change Index Scale" below was developed by Dr. Thomas Holmes and a group of researchers at the University of Washington School of Medicine. You can rate yourself by looking over the circumstances listed and marking down the index number if the situation has happened to you within the past twelve months. Add up all the points to get your total; then turn to page 188 in the appendix to interpret your score.

		Index Number
1.	Death of spouse	100
2.	Divorce	73
3.	Marital separation from mate	65
4.	Detention in jail or other institution	63
5.	Death of a close family member	63
6.	Major personal injury or illness	53
7.	Marriage	50
8.	Being fired at work	47
9.	Marital reconciliation	45
10.	Retirement from work	45
11.	Major change in the health or behavior of a family member	44
12.	Pregnancy	40
13.	Sexual difficulties	39
14.	Gaining a new family member (through birth, adoption, offspring or aging parent coming home)	39
15.	Major business readjustment (merger, reorganization, bankruptcy, etc.)	38
16.	Major change in financial state (for good or for bad)	37
17.	Death of a close friend	36
18.	Changing to a different line of work	36
19.	Change in the number of arguments with spouse (either more or less)	35
20.	Taking on a mortgage greater than $10,000 (purchasing a home, etc.)	31
21.	Foreclosure on a mortgage or loan	30
22.	Major change in responsibilities at work (promotion, demotion, transfer)	29
23.	Offspring leaving home (marriage, away to college, etc.)	29
24.	In-law problems	29
25.	Outstanding personal achievement	28
26.	Spouse beginning or ceasing work outside the home	26
27.	Beginning or ceasing formal schooling	26

■ *Danger: Brain Drain Ahead*

Most of us have had the feeling of "being put on the spot." Suddenly, you feel like your brain is mush, you can't concentrate, your heart is beating out of your chest, your blood pressure soars, and your body tenses and sweats—not a real enjoyable experience. This response, also known as stage fright, is a reaction to fear. Even though you may not be in any physical danger, your body reacts as if it is—releasing a mass of stress hormones (including cortisol) into the bloodstream. The result can be uncontrollable trembling, stammering, profuse perspiration, and a temporary loss of memory. Once you've experienced stage fright, the effect is intensified and perpetuated by the fear it will happen again.

Stage fright, as the name implies, most commonly occurs while appearing before an audience; yet, sudden embarrassment off stage can also cause a similar physical reaction. Perhaps you're unexpectedly called on in class to answer a question, or your boss singles you out in a group of your peers, or you say something you really wished you hadn't said, or you feel pressured to do something you really don't want to do. As devastating as it can feel in the moment, the effects of stage fright can be mitigated by understanding what's happening to you physiologically and learning how to offset the fear response with relaxation techniques and mental preparation.

■ 9 Tips for Conquering Stage Fright

1. Close your eyes and visualize yourself in the situation that caused the stage-fright response or that you think might cause it. Now, visualize yourself handling the situation coolly and confidently: People around you are admiring your grace and aplomb under pressure. You pull off a perfect performance. Everyone is clapping for you. You're a great success!

2. Overpractice your presentation or performance. Whatever the situation, confidence comes from a thorough understanding and knowledge of your topic or material. Use various methods of preparation. For instance, practice in front of a mirror, and in front of a friend or family member, and record yourself on video or audiotape.

3. Assemble the main points of your performance or presentation in a natural order and then associate them with images that correspond to loci-pegs (as described in Chapters 3 through 5).

4. Back up your memory with a hardcopy. Write your main points down, for instance, on index cards or on an outline. There is no shame in using visual cues. In fact, the audience will benefit from seeing how your presentation is organized, as much as you will benefit from knowing that if you forget something, all you have to do is look up.

5. Smile and speak with individual audience members or acquaintances before you go "on stage," as well as once you're there. Look at individual faces and speak directly to them, rather than to a sea of heads.

6. Ask questions of your audience. Get their minds turned inward. Everyone enjoys having things personalized for them. Plus, it takes the heat off of you.

7. If you can encourage laughter without trying too hard, you will take a huge step towards putting your audience at ease. Everyone likes to laugh spontaneously. As you make your audience feel good, you will feel good, thus perpetuating a positive exchange of energy.

8 Always speak about what you know. If you have to learn about the subject matter from beginning to end, plus prepare for a presentation, you have a lot on your plate. If you have some background experience and knowledge of a subject, you will automatically be more comfortable with it. You will be able to rely on your own experience and offer anecdotes that personalize your message.

9 Breathe deeply before you begin your presentation and continue once you're "on". As you circulate air through your lungs and body, you will naturally calm yourself. Use whatever relaxation techniques work best for you, whether it's yoga, chanting, singing, praying, walking, or mental imagery techniques.

How Is Memory Impacted by Sleep?

Beyond feeling fatigued, too little sleep is also likely to impair your concentration, judgment, reaction time, and your ability to remember things the next day. This is especially true when it comes to remembering complex information, concludes research conducted at the University de Lille in France. The mind actually depends on sleep to retain difficult memory tasks. Sleeping (and dreaming) may also help clear extraneous debris out of your memory circuits.

In-depth examinations of brain activity using PET scans during REM sleep have provided objective evidence for the theory that the dream state is important to memory. During the stage of REM sleep, which usually lasts about two hours per night, broken up into four or five twenty- to thirty-minute periods, the body becomes immobile but the brain becomes most active. PET images show that the intensive neuronal activity of REM sleep is not widespread throughout the brain, but concentrated in the AMYGDALA—crucial in the processing of emotions in waking life, the CEREBRAL CORTEX—the sensory processing station, and the entorhinal cortex—associated with long-term memory. The activation of these brain sites during REM sleep may help to explain the often powerful emotional content of dreams, their sensory aspects, and the process of "consolidating" memory traces for long-term storage that occurs during the dream state.

Bruce McNaughton of the University of Arizona and colleagues found that patterns of activity in the brains of rats performing a task are reactivated during sleep, suggesting that the sleeping rat's brain "rehearses" what it learned. The researchers surmise that when the rat performs a task, the NEOCORTEX processes sensory information and sends it to the HIPPOCAMPUS which, during sleep, initiates replay and consolidates the memory.

What Affect Does Exercise Have on Memory?

"A sedentary body makes for a sedentary mind," says Dr. Bruce Tuckman, professor of educational research at Florida State University. Numerous studies have concluded that a regular exercise program improves mental performance. Dr. Tuckman's findings come from his own research in which he discovered that school children who participated in a fifteen-week jogging program did substantially better on tests for creativity than kids who didn't exercise. A study conducted by Dr. Ted Bashore, associate professor of psychiatry at the Medical College of Pennsylvania, supports Tuckman's findings. "Aerobic exercise will not only make a difference in how your heart, lungs, and muscles function," says Dr. Bashore, "it may also make a difference in how your brain processes information"—how efficiently you make split-second decisions in the face of crisis, for example.

Studies suggest that exercise or regular physical activity can enhance mental functioning in adults and children.

Studies also suggest that adults participating in a regular aerobic exercise program experience improvements in short-term memory along with the other previously described mental benefits. In a four-month study at the Veterans Administration Medical Center in Salt Lake City Utah, psychologist Robert Dustman found that a group of sedentary adults (ages 55-70) who participated in a fast-walking program had improved neuropsychological test scores (including memory) when compared with a non-exercising control group and another group which participated in non-aerobic exercises only. Another study examined two groups of women over age sixty-five. The first group was comprised of women who exercised three times per week and the other group was comprised of women who self-rated as sedentary. Both groups were tested on their ability to estimate the speed of a sequence of flashing lights. The women who were physically active were able to better remember previous light sequences; and their ability to recall these details continued to be much stronger than the inactive women up to forty days later.

In explaining the beneficial effects of exercise on the brain, some researchers suggest that increased levels of endorphins and oxygen flow are responsible. Most recently, however, evidence points to a direct causal relationship between physical exercise and the production of a growth factor called BRAIN-DERIVED NEUROTROPHIC FACTOR (BDNF), which plays a critical role in the function and survival of NEURONS. BDNF is not only increased with exercise, but it may be selectively increased in parts of the brain associated specifically with memory formation. In addition, the greatest effects of exercise on BDNF seem to occur in the highly malleable areas of the brain implicated in degenerative age-related diseases.

Case Study

The Exercise-Memory Link

Research on successful aging suggests that physical activity (along with positive outlook and high education) is correlated with strong mental performance as people age. Scientists at the University of California, Irvine have uncovered a plausible explanation: Exercise triggers an increased production of BRAIN-DERIVED NEUROTROPHIC FACTOR (BDNF), a natural substance that was recently found to enhance neuronal communication.

When the Irvine researchers examined aging rats that had exercised daily on a running wheel, they found elevated BDNF levels in various areas of the brain, including the HIPPOCAMPUS which is critical for memory processing. BDNF has been shown to accelerate the development of LONG-TERM POTENTIATION (LTP) or memory formation in young rats. When researchers bred mice that lacked the BDNF gene, they found that the animals had markedly reduced LTP in the hippocampus. They were then able to correct the defect by reintroducing the BDNF gene into hippocampal neurons in these mice. "Our findings have potential implications for improving learning and memory in young animals and children," said researcher Bai Lu from the National Institute of Child Health and Human Development. Ira Black, a researcher at the Robert Wood Johnson Medical School, and colleagues who discovered the potential effects of BDNF on LTP, believe that the findings also offer new possibilities for studying and treating memory deficits in disorders such as Alzheimer's disease.

In What Way Does Mood Affect Memory?

Research indicates that overall memory performance can range from good to bad depending on your physical and emotional state. We all have personal experience in this department, but what specifically do you think contributes to this effect? The most obvious consideration is that if you're physically or mentally tired, your ability to pay attention suffers: We can't remember what we don't pay attention to. This simple connection between mood and memory is important when we consider how many people experience chronic fatigue, illness, and/or depression. Each of these problems over time can lead to apathy and lack of interest which may result in a withdrawal from enriching environments. Lack of enrichment impacts the physiology of our brain. We know unequivocally that our brain cells deteriorate and show fewer DENDRITIC connections when we don't challenge ourselves intellectually. Thus, excessive states of depression, exhaustion, stress, or anxiety will result in less than optimal mental functioning.

■ The Brain Out of Balance

Feeling bad for an extended period of time can also trigger a chain of physical responses that result in an imbalance of NEUROTRANSMITTERS in the brain. When our neurotransmitters, which play a key role in the acquisition, consolidation, and retrieval of memories, are thrown out of balance, memory function suffers. Depressed people frequently complain of poor memory—especially short-term memory, which is reversed when the problem is treated effectively. Returning the brain back to the proper chemical balance is the basis for the effective treatment of depression and other mood disorders.

Some researchers have also noted a link between failing short-term memory and emotional upset in the elderly. Psychosocial changes in life may account for a large part of memory problems as we age. The challenge lies in finding new activities and goals with obvious rewards when faced with a major life change. People in later life are more apt to experience loss on many levels: from the death of a spouse and/or friends and relatives to changes in physical capacity, social status, and finances. Loss on this scale can easily trigger the onset of depression, thus leading to malnutrition and further isolation. In such cases, the depression-withdrawal-chemical response cycle needs to be interrupted with an appropriate intervention.

■ *The Management of Mood States*

The irony inherent in restoring well-being with an intervention is that when you feel good, your memory for recalling positive things is improved. Once this positive state is restored, it feeds on itself. The fact that pleasurable feelings seem to act as a retrieval cue for pleasurable memories is consistent with state-dependency theory, which suggests that learning that takes place in one situation or state is generally remembered best in that same situation or state (Bower 1992; LeDoux 1996). Thus, the claim of many ancient and new-age healers, "Change your thinking and you will change your life," may be more constructive than could be empirically explained before the twentieth-century discovery of NEUROTRANSMITTERS and the intrinsic role they play in our moods and memory.

■ *Using Your Common Senses*

In his books, *Quantum Healing* and *Perfect Health*, Deepak Chopra describes the impact of our thinking and emotions on our neurochemistry. At the quantum submolecular level, your body is not a frozen sculpture of flesh and bone, but rather a dynamic flow of energy that changes from minute to minute depending on the messages relayed through your body by highly attuned chemical messengers or PEPTIDES. Your senses provide a direct link to your body's chemistry. Visual imagery, for example, can work wonders in both relaxing us and giving us the positive attitudes necessary for optimal body/mind functioning. Dr. Chopra also uses smell to heal. He explains that our sense of smell is linked directly to our brain, where it plugs into smell receptors in the HYPOTHALAMUS, a small group of cells that are involved in memory, emotion, temperature, appetite, and sexual responsiveness. Relieving emotional distress encourages physical healing. The bottom line is this: If you want to improve your memory, you have to take care of yourself mentally, as well as physically.

■ *Be Kind to Your Memory*

■ **If you believe you might be clinically depressed (or if you've been depressed for more than a few months), seek immediate advice from your physician or other health-care practitioner.**

■ **Make your nutritional needs a priority: Avoid junk foods.**

■ **Engage in physical activities suited to your degree of health and lifestyle.**

■ **If you feel unmotivated, establish a routine and stick to it.**

■ **Reestablish an old hobby you used to enjoy, or start a new one.**

- Use the skills you have to enrich the lives of those around you.

- If you've recently experienced a great loss, give yourself time and per-mission to move through the five stages of grief: shock, denial, protest/anger, depression, and eventual recovery. Learn about the grieving process with the support of friends, a support group, or professional.

- Share your experience with other people: Don't isolate yourself.

- Make a list of things you want to do in this lifetime: Start checking them off.

- Reconsider your idea of usefulness: There are many ways to find meaning in life.

- Appreciate your senses: Focus on simple things like the beauty of a sunset, the warmth of the sun on your face, a favorite old song, or your garden.

- Consider taking community education classes or going back to school.

- Set a new goal: Reawaken an old dream.

- Set a desirable mood: Light candles, play music you enjoy, take a hot bubble bath, a walk in the park, or watch an old movie.

- Learn a new relaxation or body/mind awareness technique: meditation, mind-mapping, Tai Chi, Yoga, or breathing exercises.

- Consider how unconscious attitudes may be affecting your health and life: Replace negative attitudes with positive ones.

How Is Memory Impacted by Drugs, Alcohol, and Nicotine?

Each and every substance that enters our body has some effect on our brain. In fact, the more we learn about the precarious balance of chemicals or NEURO-TRANSMITTERS that provide the communication link between our brain cells and nervous system, the more we understand the importance of reducing the potential causes of chemical imbalances in the brain. Although the brain has a built-in protection element called the BLOOD-BRAIN BARRIER, this sieve or straining mechanism is not impervious to destructive forces. In general what we find is that the average body can handle a moderate level of toxins; but as it strains to do so, it may not perform at an optimal level. When your body becomes overloaded with toxins, it is unable to keep up with the demand to rid itself of them and your immune system suffers. This state of "dis-ease" diminishes our emotional sense of well-being and our physical health. Drugs (prescription or otherwise), alcoholic beverages, and nicotine from cigarettes all are potentially toxic to your body.

■ *Memory-Sapping Drugs*

There is danger in thinking that because your doctor prescribes a medication for you or because you are able to buy it over the counter, it surely can't be bad for your brain. Numerous commonly consumed medications, such as sedatives, sleeping pills, and tranquilizers, are known to fog the mind. In addition, there are many others that, though less recognized as problematic, also have ill effects on mental functioning. Neurosurgeon Arthur Winter describes the potential effects of these medications, from Atropine to Marijuana, in his book *Brain Workout* (1997). Some classes of drugs, including sedatives or sleep medications, antidepressants, tranquilizers, antiarrhythmics or heart medications, antihypertensives or blood pressure medication, and anticonvulsants for epilepsy, have been known to cause dementia or Alzheimer's-like symptoms. Doctors point out, however, that many variables are involved in these cases such as the length of time the drug has been used, the strength of it, and the condition of the person taking it. Polypharmacy or the interaction between multiple drugs (in poorly managed patient care) can also produce effects ranging from drowsiness and feeling scattered to delayed mental functioning and slowed reaction times.

It is believed that drug-related memory impairment is caused by interruption during the memory consolidation period—the period most susceptible to influence or disruption. Although drugs may disrupt short-term memory, they don't appear to affect long-term memory. In most cases, when the problematic drug is discontinued full memory functioning returns. You should not stop taking any prescribed medications, however, without consulting your doctor. If you do have concerns regarding a drug's side effects, by all means seek the advice of a trusted health-care practitioner who will take the time to review your various medications and consider alternatives if necessary.

■ *Alcohol and Memory Awareness*

Although there are contradictions in the literature, alcohol, like caffeine, when moderately consumed seems to be handled by the body's natural-immune system well enough. The problem is that some people define "moderate" consumption as one alcoholic beverage per month, while others define it as a couple of drinks each evening. The moderation equation is further complicated by the fact that your body may be more (or less) sensitive to the effects of alcohol than others. Factors such as body weight, age, health, nutrition, water intake, speed of consumption, and alcohol content all affect how your body responds and detoxifies itself. In general, one alcoholic drink per day is not likely to affect your mental acuity. The National Institute on Alcohol Abuse and Alcoholism, however, claims that even low doses of alcohol can reduce the ability of various brain cells involved in memory to do their job. In addition, expectant mothers should completely abstain from any alcohol consumption.

People over forty are especially susceptible to alcohol-induced memory impairment—even with moderate consumption. If you pay attention to your body, it will tell you when you've crossed the line. If you experience any ill side effects: sleepiness, moodiness, impaired coordination, nausea, or forgetfulness, you have in*toxic*ated your brain. Taken further, alcohol can cause blackouts whereby whole chunks of time are literally lost from your memory. At this point you have poisoned your brain and the damage is likely irreversible.

■ *A High Price to Pay*

Studies have shown that long-term alcohol abuse actually changes the physical structure of your brain. In animal studies, after five months of alcohol consumption, pathological changes in the brain occurred including the way nerve cells conducted impulses. Human studies have shown that the brains of heavy drinkers tend to weigh less than the brains of nondrinkers and that their frontal lobes have smaller and fewer neurons. "About 75 percent of alcoholics develop brain disease," says Dr. Ralph Tarter,

Alcoholics and heavy drinkers kill off an additional 60,000 brain cells per day—60 percent more than their light-drinking or non-drinking friends.

professor of psychiatry at the University of Pittsburgh School of Medicine. "Excessive alcohol consumption destroys both neurons and glial cells causing a kind of dementia that means a permanent loss of intellectual abilities," he reports. In addition, many alcoholics experience memory loss, psychosis, and an unsteady gait as a result of thiamine deficiency.

An excessive consumption of alcohol can also age your brain prematurely. A study of forty alcoholics from age thirty to sixty revealed neuropsychological test scores on par with healthy subjects ten years older than themselves. Perhaps alcohol's most ravaging consequence, however, is the disease called Korsakoff's Syndrome. Sufferers of Korsakoff's ironically believe their memory is fine; however, upon observation and testing, it is obvious that their ability to form short-term memory is considerably impaired. They are easily distracted from a memory task and cannot recall anything that happened before they were distracted, such as the name or face of a person they met a few minutes previously. The devastating consequences that are possible as a result of drinking too much alcohol have made many a social drinker rethink the risk. If you want to safeguard your natural brain power and create the conditions for optimum memory functioning, you can't go wrong by reducing your alcohol consumption to a minimum or abstaining completely.

■ *Nicotine Contradictions*

Smoking impairs memory by constricting arteries and reducing blood flow to the brain; and *nonsmokers* score higher on standard memory tests, indicate some studies. These assertions may not surprise you. But do these? Nicotine *improves* spatial memory, learning, and information processing. Some research also suggests that nicotine *lessens* memory deficits associated with aging and Alzheimer's. Believe it or not, in spite of smoking's immensely destructive effects on a smoker's heart and lungs, some recent studies have confirmed the memory-enhancing effect of nicotine in animals and humans. The day may not be that far off when the potential benefits of nicotine may be able to be enjoyed without the toxic ill-effects that result from smoking.

■ *The High and Low of It*

Nicotine, which reaches your brain within eight seconds of inhaling it through a cigarette, affects the brain by binding to receptors that stimulate the release of NEUROTRANSMITTERS including DOPAMINE and ACETYLCHOLINE—responsible in part for mood, pleasure, and memory responses. In rat experiments, nicotine was shown to steepen the learning curve in maze-mastering exercises and to improve memory—in some cases for up to four weeks after the nicotine was administered (Levin, Rose, and Abood 1995). In human testing, nicotine has been shown to improve rapid information processing, short-term recall, spatial memory and reaction times in

The limited short-term benefit that some studies suggest nicotine provides is largely out-weighed by the long-term health threats related to smoking such as lung cancer.

Alzheimer's patients—also as a result of increased dopamine activity. For people who have wanted to quit smoking, but have not been able to kick their habit, this research may have long-term positive implications. As we gain a better understanding of the specific physiological allure of nicotine and other chemicals, we can devise more effective aids for counteracting those addictions.

Even though nicotine may provide a temporary boost in brain power, its weighty disadvantages (like the increased production of FREE-RADICALS, at best, and lung cancer at worst) clearly outweigh its limited benefit. The same advantages can be experienced by participating in healthy activities such as aerobic exercise, whereby ACETYLCHOLINE and adrenaline are triggered and also result in feelings of pleasure and relaxed alertness.

*H*ow Is Memory Impacted by Technology?

Most of us have grown so accustomed to using electronic devices, we can't fully comprehend just how dependent we are on them; nor is it easy for us to comprehend the potential impact of them on our bodies. This is why many people have never stopped to consider the warning issued by the World Health

Organization in 1984 that "Exposure to extremely low frequency electric fields (ELF) can alter cellular, physiological, and behavioral events; hence, unnecessary exposure to them should be avoided." This assertion is just the prologue of a long story that begins back in the early 1940s with Dr. Harold Saxton Burr's discovery of electrodynamic fields.

Have you ever stopped to consider the World Health Organization's 1984 warning that exposure to electromagnetic fields (EMFs) and extremely low frequency electric fields (ELFs) can alter cellular, physiological, and behavioral events; hence, unnecessary exposure to them should be avoided."

Dr. Burr, an internationally recognized neuroanatomist from Yale University, introduced the world to the idea that all living things are molded and controlled by energy fields known today as electromagnetic fields (EMFs). Since Dr. Burr's discovery, a great deal of research has been done on the effects of

EMFs on the body—during which time huge technological leaps have been made. Research has mainly focused on possible links between fatal diseases like cancer and dangerous ELFs influenced by our ever-increasing reliance on electrical appliances. The ELFs in our environment are not static but possess alternating currents pro-

Modern technologies—photography, video, audiotape, and above all the computer—restructure consciousness and memory, imposing new orders upon our understanding of the world.

—Steven Rose

The Making of Memory

ducing a magnetic field that can easily pass through the body, and may interfere with our own delicate low-frequency electromagnetic fields. It is thought that the ELFs (from household and office electronics) may be more dangerous to humans than the EMFs (from utility poles) because the ELFs resonate more closely to our own body's frequency level. In spite of these claims, the Carnegie Mellon Report recently stated that no definite link to diseases have been proven, but urged "prudent avoidance." A note of caution is appropriate here. One researcher admitted falsifying original data to create alarm.

■ *Danger: Memory Fog Ahead*

Still, a great deal of research that has focused on how our electromagnetic fields may be influenced by our thoughts and emotions, by sound and light, and by unusual solar activity, suggest that we may be more sensitive to such stimuli than we realize. Some researchers even suggest that the high exposure to ELFs and EMFs in the average big city can induce memory failure, learning disabilities, disrupted sleep patterns, a depressed immune system, cancer, and a variety of mental and behavioral disorders such as depression and hyperactivity, as changes in NEUROTRANSMITTER levels are altered. Other researchers suggest, that at the very least, powerful transmissions from TV and radio towers, high-tension electrical wires, and radiation from common household appliances, create a kind of electro-pollution or prevailing memory fog. Still, prudent avoidance, as outlined below, especially with children and while pregnant, is the general recommendation.

■ *Reducing the Risk of Electromagnetic Memory Fog*

- ■ Do not live directly under or very near to high-tension electrical wires or communication towers.
- ■ Become more aware of electricity use in your living and working environments: Reduce exposure to it wherever possible.

- Reduce the use of fluorescent lights: Utilize natural lighting as much as possible.
- Use ELF filter screens on your computer monitor. These can be purchased at most office supplies stores.
- Drink a lot of water to maintain adequate, balanced electrolyte concentration and high polarity across cellular membranes.
- Get out in nature: Walk or run or ride your bike, especially after being in front of the computer or TV for an extended period of time.
- Listen to music: It may help resynchronize the brain to its natural activity and rhythm.
- Take nutritional supplements: Research shows vitamins, minerals, and enzymes are depleted by exposure to EMFs: Sodium-potassium, hormones, and other blood chemistry balances can be affected, as well.
- Do your own research on the effectiveness of mind-machines and neuro-technical devices which claim to counteract electro-pollution and enhance brain power (see "Suggestions for Further Study" in the appendix).

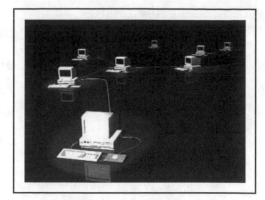

The ELFs in our environment are not static but possess alternating currents producing a magnetic field that can easily pass through the body—and interfere with our own delicate low-frequency electromagnetic fields.

Memory Booster
Lifestyle Reflection

Now that you've read this chapter, use your Memory Journal to consider what changes you might make in your life to optimize your memory fitness. Consider your degree of personal stress, the amount of sleep you get, how much you exercise, how mood impacts you, the toxins you may be ingesting, and your exposure to electro-magnetic pollution. If you want to make changes in your lifestyle, seek the advice of professionals who are trained in the specific areas you wish to improve. Getting professional support for yourself in the change process is extremely important. Remember, it took years to establish your lifestyle patterns; it may take sustained effort to change them.

Chapter Recollections

- When is stress good for learning and when is it bad?

- Would "stage fright" fall into the category of good stress or bad? Why?

- Have you experienced stage fright? What strategies have you used to overcome it? Were there other strategies in this chapter you might incorporate?

- Why is sleep important to memory?

- How does dreaming potentially influence your memory?

- What evidence suggests that exercise improves memory?

- How does lack of enrichment affect the brain?

- What factors may be influencing a reduction of memory functioning in elderly or depressed individuals who are otherwise healthy?

- What are the important factors to consider when using drugs—prescribed or otherwise?

- What are the important factors to consider when using alcohol and cigarettes? How is the brain impacted by the chemicals in these substances?

- What did you learn about EMFs and ELFs? Are you taking any precautions to avoid the effects of electro-pollution? Are there any suggestions in the chapter you might incorporate to reduce your exposure?

**What's Ahead?**

When Memory Fools or Fails Us

The Limitations of Memory

Unfortunately, countless people are serving time in our prison system for crimes they did not commit. This discouraging fact underscores the consequences of inaccurate or "false" memories. And yet, the very complexity of our memory system ensures it's susceptibility to distortion. To forget something, you only have to fail at any one of the three stages—recording, retaining, or retrieving—but to remember something you have to succeed at all three of these stages. It's a wonder we ever remember anything accurately. Even when a person's memory seems to be distorted, they may be accurately recalling what was encoded into it.

If this complex network called memory is made up of feelings, moods, thoughts, words, sensory perceptions, emotions, imagination, and intellect, can we expect it to be impervious to influence and interpretation? Of course not! Even two people waiting in line next to each other when a bank is held up will often provide contradictory eyewitness statements. There are numerous explanations for this and other phenomenon that make our memories seem like fickle friends. This chapter summarizes the inherent fallibility of our memory system and examines the quality of memories under various conditions, such as when faced by trauma, suggestion, depression, aging, and disease. The implications of this work are as deep and profound as the commitment of the scientists who have devoted their life's work to its study.

*H*ow Accurate Are Our Memories?

There are two primary types of memories, implicit and explicit—the first being more fixed, while the latter is less so. Implicit memories, which include procedural learning, like skill training or physical habits; emotional encoding, like traumas, phobias, or other intense sensory experiences; and stimulus-response learning, like rhymes, faces, and flashcards, all seem to change little over time. Explicit memories, however, which we consciously rely on the most—ones full of content, data, facts, locations and events—are highly subjective and malleable.

Elizabeth Loftus, a leading authority in eyewitness testimony and memory distortion, explains that memory traces do not remain intact, but undergo changes with time and external influences (1980). "We literally construct and reconstruct memories each time we recall them—either reinforcing the memory trace with some new association or weakening it by neglecting to recall it," she reports. Even if the memory trace is strong to begin with, it is vulnerable to all sorts of contaminating influences, such as another person's opinion, subliminal suggestion, misperception, and distraction. Judges in high-profile cases know the importance of protecting jurors' from memory contamination; thus, sequestering a jury is common practice in highly publicized cases.

> **We need to recognize** that memories do not exist in one of two states—either true or false—and that the important task is to examine how and in what ways memory corresponds to reality.
>
> —Daniel L. Schacter
> *Searching for Memory*

The biological explanation for memory subjectivity is that each time we retrieve a memory we activate a field or web of neuronal connections (see Chapter 1; figure 1.4). These connections between cells link axons to dendrites. The brain cells that were activated during the original learning "fired" together and, thus, are "wired" together. Usage strengthens these connections, while disuse weakens them. Misuse can create new, sometimes inaccurate, connections; and abuse can alter or destroy the connections altogether. In short, the fragile connections that give us the "wiring" for much of our semantic (factual) and episodic (experiential) retrieval are highly modifiable.

The Construction of Memory

The influences that can distort a person's recall are numerous: 1) a missing retrieval cue; 2) decay or disuse; 3) interference or exposure to new learning that wipes out the old; 4) repression; 5) priming or suggestion; and 6) perception or experience. Any of these factors can interfere with the original memory trace and thus, influence a false memory. But can a false memory be totally invented, or is it more likely that a true memory becomes distorted? Experiments have shown that simply repeating a false statement enough times leads people to believe it is true. Studies conducted with siblings have demonstrated that when one sibling fakes a memory involving the other, more often than not, the second sibling begins to recall details of the "virtual" incident, as well. These cases suggest that our memory is highly susceptible to influence; and in fact, can be "constructed" in our own heads by another person. The fact of the matter is, explicit memories are highly modifiable.

The famous Swiss psychologist Jean Piaget recounted a poignant experience from his own childhood that informed his thoughts on the nature of false memory. For years he believed he had been kidnapped as a toddler. He remembered the traumatic incident in great detail: the street on which it occurred, the man snatching him away from his caretaker, and her fighting off the attacker until a uniformed officer arrived on the scene. It was not until Piaget was a teenager that he learned that, in fact, the incident had never happened. The nanny admitted years later that she had fabricated the story as a ploy to impress young Piaget's wealthy parents. What Piaget truly remembered was *accounts* of the incident, which he had visualized in surprising detail. Over time, the memory was as real to him as anything. The ability to construct memory (whether it is self- or other-induced) has been demonstrated time and again. From high-profile sex scandals to televised murder trials, powerful public figures spotlighted by the media highlight just how illusive the search for truth can be.

The Case of the Missing Retrieval Cue

To record a memory your brain first perceives a stimulus and encodes it in the appropriate location; to retrieve the memory, a cue or second stimulus leads you back to the memory network. Thus, we tend to remember things we recorded in a particular mood when we are in the same mood (state-dependency); likewise, our recall of information increases when the retrieval cue is accessible. If the retrieval cue is inaccessible, so is the memory. This is why going back to the scene of a crime is a good way to induce eyewitness memory. Most of us have experienced the recovery of a retrieval cue prompted by simply returning to the prior setting. The next time you kick yourself for recalling the answer to a test question after the test is over, realize it was a matter of a missing retrieval cue. Retrieval cues can be conscious or unconscious.

Consider how often you rely on unconscious cues to jog your memory when driving. On my way to the office, the flashing yellow warning lights automatically cue me to merge right for a turn that always comes up fast. The bridge signals that my exit is the next one. Conscious cues are very helpful, as well. Directions that include statements like, turn

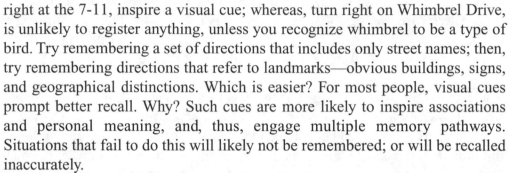

It is not so astonishing, the number of things I can remember, as the number of things I can remember that aren't so.

—Mark Twain

right at the 7-11, inspire a visual cue; whereas, turn right on Whimbrel Drive, is unlikely to register anything, unless you recognize whimbrel to be a type of bird. Try remembering a set of directions that includes only street names; then, try remembering directions that refer to landmarks—obvious buildings, signs, and geographical distinctions. Which is easier? For most people, visual cues prompt better recall. Why? Such cues are more likely to inspire associations and personal meaning, and, thus, engage multiple memory pathways. Situations that fail to do this will likely not be remembered; or will be recalled inaccurately.

◼ *The Evil Twins: Inattention and Distraction*

We don't necessarily internalize all that we see. In fact, much of the sensory information we're bombarded with minute-by-minute is ignored—out of necessity. We can't possibly process all that life throws at us on a conscious level. Encoding information is not necessarily automatic, particularly when we are attending to internal matters that distract us from external stimuli.

It follows then that being at the scene of a crime does not, by any means, guarantee eyewitness accuracy. The most obvious explanation for this is that the attention of the "witness" may not have been focused on the particulars they're later questioned about. Lack of attention is, in fact, the main reason we so often forget things—the names of people we've just been introduced to, where we left our keys, or what color shirt a person was wearing, as well as other types of information that might be crucial, for instance, in a court of law. Those of us who commute to work each day know how easy it is to fall into "auto-pilot" mode, where the time that passes gets lost in implicit (nonconscious) memory. The only way to fight absentmindedness is to make yourself aware of the distractions that come between you and your goal and refuse to give into them. If you're on the way to water the plants, for example, and are distracted by the dog wanting to be fed, recognize the interference, but bypass it for the moment. Author and memory trainer Danielle Lapp (1987) calls this the "one-track mind technique."

*D*oes Memory Fade or Decay?

Although most psychologists believe that long-term memories are permanently stored in the mind even if they aren't necessarily accessible, some neurobiological research with invertebrate organisms has shown that the neural changes that underlie some simple forms of memory weaken and even disappear over time. This finding supports the decay or "wax tablet" theory of forgetting, which Plato conceived when he wrote, "As we remember, we etch lines and patterns in the soft surface; then time—the great eraser—slowly smoothes the lines away, causing us to forget."

The curve of forgetting, in fact, may be so great as to be depressing. The nineteenth century German psychologist Hermann Ebbinghaus, who is credited with early empirical findings on the classification and nature of memory, determined just how much exposure was needed to remember a series of nonsense syllables. From this and other studies, the Ebbinghaus Curve (figure 8.1) was charted, which as you'll see below, suggests that over half of new information learned or assimilated is already forgotten one hour later; and a month later, 80 percent of it has evaporated (Ebbinghaus 1964). One key to memory accuracy, therefore, may be its timely retrieval. This is why repetition in learning is so important. A positive way of looking at the curve is that what you still remember after fifteen hours pass, you'll likely remember for a long time, if not indefinitely.

Figure 8.1

The Ebbinghaus Curve

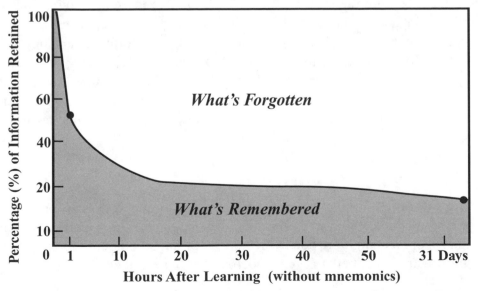

■ Memory Interference

Simply overhearing others talk about an incident can influence your memory of it, just as later events can change your memory of earlier events. For example, I found out recently that one of my previous colleagues (whom I liked very much and held fond memories of) was indicted for grand auto theft. This new information has caused me to re-evaluate how much I really liked him. Now, I recall how he really wasn't all that trustworthy. The present information has "contaminated" or interfered with my past memory.

Ebbinghaus' work, which related how time influences forgetting was important; but psychologists have since identified confounding factors that also influence accuracy, such as interference or competing stimuli subsequent to the original memory. Interference can come in a host of forms—it might be information you gleaned from the newspaper, a neighbor, or a conversation overheard while dining out. The interference theory suggests that a new experience or learning can "cancel out" the old, or at least, cause confusion; and the more similar the experiences or memories, the more likely it is that the newer memory will interfere. Often the result is source-memory confusion—that is, we lose track of how our memory has been influenced by subsequent events. If I ask you, for example, what you had for dinner last night, you can probably retrieve the memory without too much trouble, right? But, what if I asked you what you had for dinner a week ago, Thursday? It is unlikely that you will remember this as easily because, the theory goes, many similar memories have since interfered.

The interference takes place because all of your *what* memories (like *what* you had for dinner) are stored simultaneously with your *where* memories (like *where* you ate the dinner). Every *what* you've learned in your life was connected to a *somewhere*. However, the more unique, relevant, and meaningful the event (like a celebration or crisis), the more easily that memory can be elicited. The more contaminated the event is by similar or repeated memories, the more difficult it becomes to elicit a specific memory. To use a computer analogy, let's say that you've given each of your files a unique address (file name) as is common practice so that you can later identify what's what. But now a virus gets into your computer and gives all of your files the same name. The data remains intact, but how do you now locate it? This is how interference operates in our memory system.

■ Emotional Memories

The flip side of forgetting things we don't pay attention to, don't use, or that are canceled out by interference, is remembering things that engage our emotions. Do most people retain more potent memories of traumatic or emotional events? Yes, but we are much better at remembering that the event occurred than being accurate about its details. A study by psychologist Ulric Neisser (1992) revealed, that in fact, only a .29 correlation existed between confidence of recall and accuracy about a memorable occurrence (in this case, the 1986 Challenger disaster). Still life-changing occasions like getting married, the birth of a child, or a family member's death; and firsts like our first bike, puppy dog, car, kiss, or break-up are chemically marked in our memories as neurotransmitters surge in response to the significance of these events.

Strong emotional memories (like the love of a favorite childhood pet) remain vital—although not necessarily accurate—due to the priority attention emotions receive when being processed and stored by the brain.

Strong emotional memories are stored more easily because they are unique or at least more novel; and thus travel a more direct pathway in the brain. While interesting facts or enjoyable occurrences may be processed by the HIPPOCAMPUS and stored in the TEMPORAL LOBES, emotional memories begin in the THALAMUS (like other non-emotional memories), but are likely shuttled to the AMYGDALA for immediate action (safety or survival) and long-term storage.

Researchers point out, however, that in very unexpected, violent, or confusing situations like an earthquake, terrorist attack, or plane crash, witnesses are bombarded with sensory stimuli practically guaranteeing that the person will forget aspects of the experience. This distinction is important because there seems to be a break point between emotional stress and traumatic stress. Where emotional intensity may be marked by the release of GLUCOCORTICOIDS (including cortisol) tagging it as unique and important and memorable; traumatic or prolonged stress can result in a type of "cortisol-poisoning."

Over time, an overabundance of cortisol released in response to prolonged stress kills brain cells. As described in Chapter 7, studies of the long-term effects of glucocorticoids suggest that physical changes begin to occur in the hippocampus, a brain region important for learning and memory, in response to major stresses or prolonged exposure to elevated cortisol levels. Clinical depression, post-traumatic stress disorder, and physiological malfunction are also major causes of excessive cortisol circulation in the body. Figure 8.2 on page 165 provides a visual synopsis of the changes that occur in an aging or stressed brain, and how they can be avoided or minimized.

What Happens to Traumatic Memories?

Memories that were accompanied by great stress and intensity are usually linked to strongly felt associations which helped us survive the threatening circumstances. Particularly when danger is perceived, the brain's higher-order thinking centers are bypassed to ensure a faster response—usually referred to as "fight or flight" phenomenon. Danger seems to get encoded along a more direct pathway to the brain and often results in reflexive behaviors that can last a lifetime. For example, the person who was attacked by a Rottweiler as a child will most likely be afraid of them for a very long time (if not forever), unless desensitized or "retrained."

Fear is the strongest of all emotional memories; however, other emotions, such as disappointment, frustration, or sadness, can also trigger implicit (subconscious) memories that evoke intense responses. Therapists today are finding new ways of using mind technology to release traumas that have been stored in the body-mind. Many of their findings can be explained in terms of the mind-body therapy of Wilhelm Reich, who over fifty-five years ago pointed out how traumatic experiences are stored away in the body as habitual muscular tensions and neuromuscular patterns he called "body armor." We now know that, in fact, traumatic events become translated into neuro-PEPTIDES and other "intelligent" chemicals, which then circulate through the body making permanent changes on a cellular level.

In many instances, traumatic memories may develop into phobias and other persistent "illogical" behaviors. As such, we may not seem to be behaving in very rational ways when such memories are triggered. The result can be inappropriate responses for the current context. Sometimes referred to as "emotional baggage" or "toxic memories," these associations can end up interfering with current relationships and healthy communication patterns if we don't acknowledge their existence and consciously replace obsolete responses with more appropriate ones.

■ Repressed Memories

What's peculiar about this kind of memory is that most traumatic memories (not all) are stored implicitly. This means that while we respond to them in the moment, we may never attach language to them. Often we were too young, too afraid, or too confused to even tell anyone about them. Our body, however, knows about the trauma—even if our language pathways have never put the memories into words. Often what we call repressed memories are simply unspoken memories. It may have been too painful or difficult to share them.

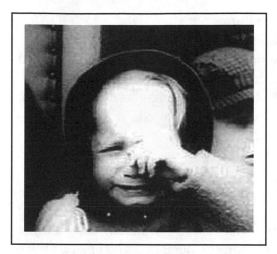

Endorphins (and other glucocorticoids) may act as memory blockers providing a protective mechanism, known as repression, which aids survival in the face of unbearable mental or physical pain.

Describing them in words can feel like an impossible task, especially if the memories originated before language was acquired. This is when a good therapist can be invaluable to help unravel the images and feelings. Once we attach language to the trauma, it can be dissected and understood so that a path towards healing begins.

A national survey conducted by the School of Medicine at the University of California, Los Angeles found that while most survivors of trauma—60 percent—be it childhood sexual abuse, military combat, street violence, or natural disaster, clearly remembered their experiences, while 40 percent suffered periods of total or partial amnesia. An explanation for such forgetting was first suggested by Sigmund Freud. He called it repression and described it as a conscious exclusion of a traumatic event from the conscious mind. Though Freud documented the phenomenon in a great number of patients, only recently has a possible biological link to repression been identified. Studies conducted by Michela Gallagher at the University of North Carolina suggest that GLUCOCORTICOIDS may play an important role in the biological mechanism of repression and remembering. They may act as memory blockers, as well as pain blockers, providing a natural protective mechanism for survival in the face of unbearable mental or physical pain.

■ *The Repression/Recovery Controversy*

Psychologist Elizabeth Loftus (1994) argues that while some people may indeed temporarily repress and later retrieve memories of bygone abuse, there is little scientific evidence to support total memory oblivion. In spite of notable reports in the past decade or so of individuals who have "recovered" long-forgotten memories of horrific abuse at the hands of a family member or trusted adult, most repressed memories are not completely forgotten, she contends. As evidenced by the persistent memories of holocaust survivors and war veterans, even when a person wants to forget traumatic memories, circumstances unwittingly trigger them over time virtually guaranteeing their existence to some degree.

The place in the brain that traumatic memories are stored, the AMYGDALA appears to store emotional memories forever (LeDoux 1996). This impressive almond-shaped structure holds what some have called "our stored emotional wisdom." It is the repository of every strong emotional event that has ever occurred in our lives. And since many of those events may have had a link to some kind of survival activity, it's good we have them stored. As such, it is very difficult for many in the field to believe that a total blanking out of a traumatic experience or repetitive trauma is possible.

The extent to which repression can occur marks a spirited debate among the psychiatric and therapeutic communities. On one side of the debate are those who believe that multiple-event trauma victims may experience a definite "hole" in their memory which occurs as a natural mental survival mechanism. Such "robust repression," is believed to be so deep in the psyche that it is virtually unrecoverable through explicit memory pathways. Believers in the robust repression theory often advocate "therapeutic retrieval" techniques (including hypnosis) to "recover" the implicit memory traces buried deep in the unconscious.

On the other side of the debate are those who feel that highly suggestible people can easily be encouraged by unscrupulous therapists to "remember" events that never took place. Memory is highly susceptible to suggestion and the desire to locate explanations for mental stress can be so strong that causes can literally be invented. Psychologists who are skeptical of robust repression are also quick to point out that they are not discrediting the memories of child-abuse victims, nor standard therapeutic protocol in the healing of abuse survivors—only the seemingly impossible total memory repression pre-psychotherapy and memory recovery post-psychotherapy that has emerged of late.

The most difficult of these cases to reconcile are the ones in which adults "recover" memories that they had no pre-therapy inclination of, no physical evidence of trauma, no collaborating witnesses, and no psychological disturbances or anti-social behavior reported during the abuse years or later. Combined with a complete lack of telltale signs, "recovered" memories can be most perplexing when they include the most lurid of allegations. You may remember the McMartin case during the late-1980s in which the owners of a Southern California preschool were indicted on multiple counts of child abuse. The trial became one of the most notorious and expensive cases ever tried. The McMartin family was eventually exonerated of all charges; and the children's testimony of lurid sexual abuse was later discredited. Nevertheless, a family's livelihood, their reputation, and their resources were destroyed in what has become a classic case of false/recovered memories.

In the discussion of child abuse, however, psychologist are quick to acknowledge the great value of psychotherapy techniques performed by scrupulous professionals with abuse victims who report personal spontaneous memory of the trauma.

Case Study

From Psychologist to Rapist: A Case of Mistaken Source Memory

In an ironic incident reported by Daniel Schacter, author of *Searching for Memory*, we can see just how devastating source-memory confusion can potentially be. In this case, a respected psychologist Donald Thompson, whose subject specialty was memory distortion, was wrongly identified by a rape victim as her attacker. It's not difficult to imagine how Thompson must have felt in the face of such an accusation, even though he had an air-tight alibi. It turns out that Thompson had been conducting an interview on live television just before the rape occurred. It later came to light that just prior to the rape, the victim had been watching the TV show where Thompson was ironically describing how people could improve their memory for faces.

Once it was recognized that the woman had confused the face of the rapist with her memory of Thompson from the television interview, he was released immediately. This scary mistake points out just how fallible source memory is. The failure to remember the correct source of acquired information is responsible, in fact, for many kinds of errors and distortions in eyewitness recollections and other aspects of everyday memory, reports Schacter.

How Much Are We Influenced By the Power of Suggestion?

In classic eyewitness memory studies conducted by Elizabeth Loftus and her colleagues (1974), subjects were shown slides depicting a car collision subsequent to its entry into an intersection after pausing at a stop sign. After witnessing the event, some of the subjects were asked, "What happened to the car after it stopped at the *stop* sign?" Others were asked a purposely misleading question: "What happened to the car after it stopped at the *yield* sign?" Later, everyone was asked whether the car came to a halt at a *stop* or *yield* sign.

People who had been asked the misleading question tended to remember having seen a yield sign. The researchers argue that the misleading suggestion effectively wiped out any memory of the existing stop sign.

Psychologists point out, however, that other studies suggest misleading information may not necessarily eliminate the original memory, but induce a source memory problem—confusion about what was actually coded in the original memory versus information added to the memory subsequently. In other words, the person becomes unable to identify from what "source" the memory originated. This can make for some very confusing recollections, which is especially problematic in the case of courtroom testimonies. A person can feel extremely confident in the accuracy of their memory and yet, it is really a memory composite, flawed by contamination.

■ *Priming*

Another form of suggestion which can influence what is remembered is called priming. Priming is the offering of selected content immediately (seconds or minutes) prior to the retrieval event. Research suggests that words (and presumably other sensory input) can be unconsciously cued into the memory of a subject by exposure (Tulving, Schacter 1990). Priming is sometimes used when police pressure is applied to eyewitnesses and suspected criminals. Lawyers use it when they ask leading questions. And parents use it to channel their children's energy in particular directions. Priming is best demonstrated by Daniel Schacter's (1996) example which follows:

Study each of the following words carefully for five seconds: assassin, octopus, avocado, mystery, sheriff, and climate. Now imagine that you go about your business for an hour and then return to take a couple of tests, during which you are shown a series of words and asked whether you remember seeing any of them previously. The words are: *twilight, assassin, dinosaur,* and *mystery.* You probably remember that *assassin* and *mystery* were on the prior list. Next, you are told that you will be shown some words with missing letters. Your job is to fill in the blanks as best you can:

ch - - - - nk   **o - t - - us**   **- og - y - - -**   **- l - m - te**

Let us guess what happened. You *probably* had a hard time coming up with a correct answer for the two word fragments, *chipmunk* and *bogeyman*, right? The correct answers to the other two, *octopus* and *climate*, however, probably jumped right out at you. The reason for this may be obvious. You were primed with the words *octopus* and *climate* in the list of study words. Just seeing the words on the list seems to prime our subconscious. This exercise illustrates just how easily we're influenced by suggestion, subliminal or not. The propensity to adopt or adapt a memory inaccurately is called CRYPTOMNESIA.

Examples of priming are all around us. Perhaps, the suggestion you made to your boss a month ago (that seemed to be ignored) has suddenly resurfaced as his idea. Before you bang him over the head with your fattest dictionary, consider that he may have unintentionally infringed on your idea. The fact of the matter is, such infringement happens all the time—purposefully and not. Lawyers commonly use this strategy to influence the memory of a witness. The question, "What color was the attacker's hat?" may cause the witness to remember a hat that did not exist. Advertising campaigns also take advantage of our implicit (unconscious memory)—sometimes referred to as subliminal seduction. Thus, the next time you get hungry while watching TV, check out your motivation before you make a midnight "run to the border."

■ *You're Never Too Young to Be Primed*

Studies with prelinguistic infants and even newborns suggest that babies develop a "preference" for their mother very early on. Using a procedure in which newborns can control the sounds they hear by sucking on a non-nutritive nipple, it has been demonstrated that a three-day-old infant will suck more frequently when hearing the sound of its mother's voice over an unfamiliar one. Has the infant registered an implicit memory of their mother's voice in utero? Perhaps. In another study in which women repeatedly read aloud a Dr. Seuss story during the final six weeks of pregnancy, the newborns showed through sucking that they preferred to listen to their mothers telling the familiar story versus a story they had never heard before. Now, we must consider that it's not just Mother's voice the infant is recalling. Whether these cases speak of the power of priming or something else, they demonstrate the involuntary nature of implicit memory. This subtle form of influence may help explain more than a newborn's preference for what it knows; it may enlighten us as to our own personal biases (see also Chapter 5: for more on children and memory).

The first sensory stimulation we receive is in utero. Studies conducted with newborns suggest we "remember" these sensations or, at least, are primed to recognize (prefer) them soon after birth.

■ *Perception*

Every bit of information we perceive with our senses is added to our personal palette of experience and constitutes our frame of reference. This perceptual filter, thus, colors all of our interpretations. This is one reason why the memories of the same event can vary so widely among eyewitnesses. The human mind is so sophisticated that it continually fills in the blanks of an incomplete image, scene, or scenario automatically and unconsciously based on past experience.

David Rumelhart of the University of California, San Diego demonstrates how our perception filters operate in the following simple scenario. Consider the following two unremarkable sentences:

> *Mary heard the ice-cream truck coming down the street. She remembered her birthday money, and ran into the house.*

Rumelhart explains that "most people recognize that Mary is a little girl, that she wants ice cream when she hears the truck, and that she goes into the house to get money in order to buy some ice cream." Perhaps this is obvious, but where in these two sentences does it actually say any of these things? "Most people," he expounds, "add or fill in the missing material by making a set of inferences that draw upon their personal stockpile of world knowledge" (Hunt 1983). It is through these associative networks of memory that we recognize variations of patterns or symbols. Consider the role your perceptual powers play as you interpret the following images.

What do you see when you look at these distorted images?

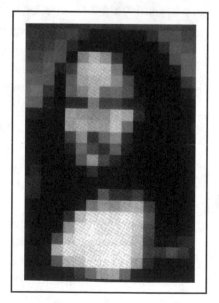 

Turn to page 162 for confirmation.

Memory Workout

A Prime Example (Try this out!)

Start by taking a minute to read and pay careful attention to the following series of words:

candy · sour · sugar · bitter · good · taste · tooth · nice · honey · soda · chocolate · heart · cake · eat · pie

Now cover the words and write down as many of them as you can remember before going on to the next step.

_____

_____

With the above section still covered, try to remember if any of the following three words appeared on the list: **taste, point, sweet**. Now, consider whether you actually remember *seeing* them on the list; and assess how confident you are in your recall. The majority of people who participate in this exercise recall that two out of the three words above were on the list. But, actually, only **taste** was on the list; **sweet**, however, is usually falsely remembered. Why? The explanation for it is actually rather obvious. Each of the words on the original list held some association with the word **sweet**, which likely activates the category of "sweet things" in your mind. This exercise, developed in the 1950s, has demonstrated time and time again the same results—most people not only believe that *sweet* was on the list but claim to remember it vividly (Schacter 1996).

■ *Fact or Fiction: A Look Inside the Brain*

Recent studies conducted by Eric Reiman of the Good Samaritan Medical Center in Phoenix and Harvard professor Daniel Schacter have demonstrated how brain activity underlying accurate and mistaken memory for recently spoken words has been differentiated in some cases on PET scans. Although, follow-up studies have suggested there may be more similarities than differences, these results are very promising in that distinct brain location activity has been identified when people accurately remembered previously spoken words. It is too soon to draw conclusions about the veracity of a person's recall based on the activity in the brain, caution the researchers. Even so, one can't help but speculate that these positive findings may increase the interest in and plausibility of developing electronic devices for measuring memory accuracy. The implications of such a development would truly be profound.

What happened when you observed the distorted images on page 160, now in focus above? Did your incredibly efficient memory fill in the blanks quite automatically? More than likely it did, demonstrating how our brain makes unconscious contextual interpretations moment by moment. Sir Frederic Bartlett wrote in his 1932 publication, *Remembering*, that "the experience of remembering may be shaped as much by the rememberer's attitude, expectations, and general knowledge regarding what should and could have happened as by the content of specific past events." This paradox is demonstrated in the Memory Workout on the previous page.

*W*hat Is the Truth About Memory Loss?

A survey by the Dana Foundation found that 67 percent of adults surveyed worried about memory loss. Diminished memory can be caused by many things: poor nutrition, a head injury, a nervous system disorder, a brain tumor, drug or alcohol abuse, prescription medication, anxiety or depression, excess CORTISOL released in response to sustained stress, estrogen withdrawal in menopause, or the general passage of time. Considering all the possibilities, identifying the cause of memory loss can be a tricky business. Thus, many people lump their memory challenges into the catch-all called "old age." An anecdote often heard these days is "Oh, please excuse me, I'm having a senior moment." Although, our memory does change as we age like other biological processes, certainly more memory failure is blamed on aging than recent scientific findings warrant.

The Passage of Time

Although the brain can and does grow some new cells throughout life, a reduction in DENDRITIC branching, oxygen deprivation, and cell damage in the HIPPOCAMPUS over time can result in diminished memory. This natural decay may partly explain why our memory fades and becomes gradually less accessible over time. Structurally fewer connections are made in the brain as a result of less novelty and enrichment, while memory potential not supported by exercise, usage, and good nutrition suffers as well.

Beyond this gradual physical breakdown, another cause of normal forgetting may be that as time passes, we encode and store new experiences that interfere with our ability to recall previous ones. Thus, by virtue of time on the planet, an older person will have more interference and increased forgetfulness. Although many of the circumstances affiliated with mild memory loss may occur more often in the elderly, other than a mild slowing down of metabolic processes in normal aging, your memory is not necessarily destined for doom in your sunset years.

Psychological Stress and Depression

Psychological disturbance is more detrimental to memory than most people realize. Sustained stress, anxiety, grief, emotional trauma, and depression are all bad guys in the war on forgetfulness. Anxiety in response to something like giving a speech, taking a difficult exam, losing one's job, or making a major life change can temporarily decrease our memory, but it is the insidious stress sustained over an extended period of time that is more serious. For example, the person who continues to work in a distressing environment year after year when they know "it is killing them," is right. It is killing their brain cells! (see Chapter 7; figure 7.1). Children who live in dysfunctional families often experience memory difficulties, which understandably results in problems with schoolwork as semantic learning takes a backseat to survival learning. At any age, significant memory problems can develop as a result of any emotional disturbances or long-term depression. When living in an extreme emotional state, most people pay less attention to the outside world and more attention to their internal strife and pain. And yet, in order to remember something, we have to pay attention to it. The good news is that full memory functioning often returns when the stress or depression in a person's life is reduced or eliminated. Therapeutic treatments now available for anxiety and depression have helped many reclaim their memory prowess.

Remember...
a Reduction in Memory
Performance May Be a Result of:

- **Passivity or mindlessness**
- **Short attention span**
- **Lack of interest or motivation**
- **Lack of sensory awareness**
- **Lack of need (or perceived need)**
- **Reduced physical/mental energy**
- **Reduced use of mental imagery**
- **Difficulty in focusing or concentrating**
- **Intense stress or anxiety**
- **Depression**
- **Nutritional inadequacies**
- **Drugs, medications, or alcohol**
- **Estrogen withdrawal in menopause**
- **Physical injury or disease**

Figure 8.2

As We Age:
How and Where Our Memory Changes

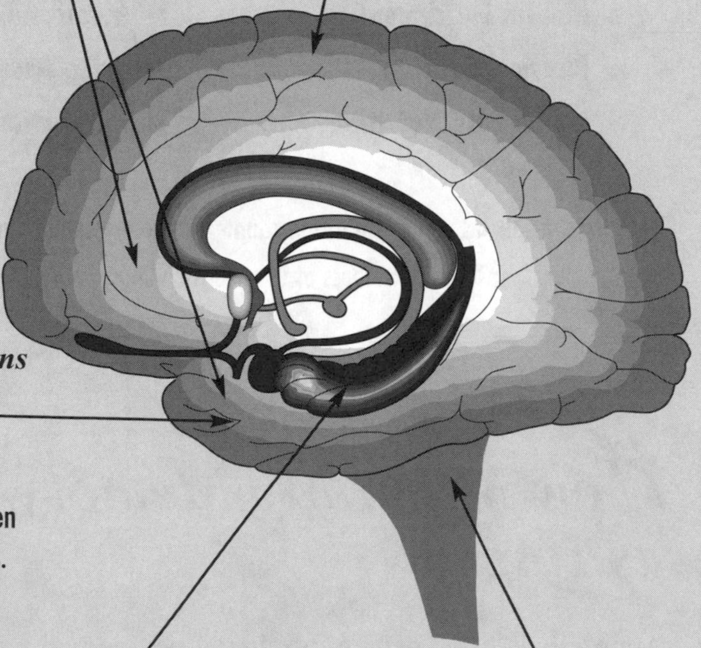

Brain damage to key memory circuits may occur
Solutions:
Provide head protection; increase safety, reduce toxins, and add memory supplements.

Brain cells may receive less oxygen
Solutions:
Increase cardiovascular activity.

Temporal lobe connections may weaken due to lack of enrichment
Solutions:
Rely on your memory more often and increase mental challenges.

Neurons in the hippocampus may die off in response to prolonged stress
Solutions:
Reduce stress by using daily relaxation strategies.

Neurotransmitter production may drop
Solutions:
Increase dietary nutrition, especially nutrients that trigger the production of key memory neurotransmitters.

Memory Booster
Journal Activity

If you've been keeping a memory journal, by now you've probably identified some of your basic memory strengths and weaknesses. In your journal, consider each of the following lifestyle factors that impact memory performance and discuss how they may or may not apply to you:

- **Intense Emotions**
- **Depression**
- **Major Life Change(s)**
- **Mental Enrichment**
- **Physical Exercise**
- **Inadequate Nutrition**

- **Sustained Stress or Trauma**
- **Fatigue or Anxiety**
- **Unchanging Routines**
- **Medications, Drugs, or Alcohol**
- **False Assumptions**
- **Distraction**

Brainstorm strategies you might use to counteract these common memory diminishers (i.e., pausing to increase conscious awareness of your surroundings, taking a visual snapshot, etc.).

*H*ow Might My Memory Change as I Age?

Approximately 25 percent of elderly people will basically show no change in their memory from when they were young. Five percent will thrive at genius level well into their 90s, like the twentieth century British philosopher Bertrand Russell. And, of the remaining 70 percent who exhibit some memory change, about 10 to 20 percent will suffer from what's called AGE-ASSOCIATED MEMORY IMPAIRMENT or MILD COGNITIVE IMPAIRMENT (MCI). Thus, most of us will probably have to deal with some age-consistent memory changes as we get older and our perception of time slows down. The physiological changes we experience as we age, however, depend on multiple factors including exercise, nutrition, continuing mental stimulation, willingness to try new things, and attitude.

In studies conducted since the 1970s, scientists have discovered that lack of use may be more detrimental to memory than aging itself. In other words, a seventy-year-old who has continued to learn and study may actually be more mentally fit than a forty-year-old who has neglected their mental fitness. Research has shown that factors such as number of years of schooling and current enrollment in classes are both positively related to memory ability. These factors also correlated positively to the usage of memory techniques or MNEMONICS in middle-aged women—which we would presume also improves memory performance. The bottom line is this: Adults who remain mentally active by maintaining reading and studying habits are better able able to recall what they read than adults who do not stay mentally active. Memory peeks at approximately age sixteen and begins to decline slightly (up to about 30 percent) over the remaining lifespan. But there are wide differences in normal memory decline as we age: and practice, meaning, and importance play a crucial role in these differences.

Marion Perlmutter, who has been studying memory in aging people (1978a), has found that people in their sixties and up definitely

Scientists have discovered that lack of use may be more detrimental to memory than aging itself; and that adults who remain mentally active (with problem-solving activities such as crossword puzzles, chess, bridge, etc.) perform better on cognitive tests than their less challenged peers.

recall and recognize lists of words less well than people in their twenties; however, the older set recalls and recognizes facts better. This finding underscores the importance of associations to memory. The older we are, presumably the more complex and comprehensive are our associative networks; and thus, our chances of remembering facts. A healthy adult adapts to his/her environment in amazingly effective ways: If great demand is placed on our memory, we find ways to remember. It is true, however, that some types of memory may be more impacted by aging than others. For example, my grandmother at age ninety could remember the exact date of every important occasion her family ever celebrated; and yet, she regularly forgot to turn off household appliances. A diminishing ability to remember names and what's called MULTI-TASKING—doing more than one thing at a time or being interrupted and still remembering it all—is common in the senior years. The phone rings, for example, while preparing a casserole; and when you return, you've forgotten whether you added the final ingredient. The good news is, however, that memory (of any kind) can be improved at any age so long as a person can understand and practice the type of memory strategies outlined in this book.

What Diseases Impair Memory?

When significant impairment in two or more cognitive domains (i.e., language, memory, and personal planning) is experienced—and the impairment is severe enough to interfere with daily functioning—the decline is called dementia. Dementia can be caused by multiple strokes, a brain tumor, Korsakoff's Syndrome (related to alcoholism) or the leading cause—Alzheimer's disease. "Many years ago, when people lost their memory and became senile as they aged, it was thought that this was a natural effect of getting older," reports Dr. Mark Alberts, a neurologist at the Alzheimer's Disease Research Center at Duke University Hospital. "But we know now that senility is not a normal function of aging. It's not normal to get to be seventy or eighty and not be able to understand and remember things. That's clearly abnormal."

■ The Who, What, and Where of Alzheimer's Disease

Half of us who reach the age of eighty-five will suffer from Alzheimer's disease, reports Dr. Robert Green, a Georgia State University neurologist and head of the University's Alzheimer's research, diagnostic, and treatment program. The disease, which is chronic and fatal, can strike anyone. Presently, 10 percent of people over the age of sixty-five and four million people overall in the United States are experiencing the progressive loss of mental faculties associated with Alzheimer's. Sadly, this number is expected to multiply as baby boomers age and life-expectancy rates expand.

Half of us who reach the age of eighty-five will suffer from Alzheimer's disease, which is chronic, fatal, and can strike anyone. Presently, 10 percent of people over the age of sixty-five and four million people overall in the United States are experiencing the progressive loss of mental faculties associated with Alzheimer's.

The disease primarily affects the HIPPOCAMPUS, a structure largely responsible for cognition and memory located in the mid-brain area, but it also attacks nerve cells in all parts of the CEREBRAL

CORTEX. Characterized by irreversible memory loss, disorientation, speech problems, balance problems, and intellectual decline, Alzheimer's disease lasts between three and fifteen years before the patient dies. It is the fourth leading cause of death among the elderly (after heart disease, cancer, and stroke). German neurologist Alois Alzheimer, who bears the disease's name, first described neurofibrillary tangles (abnormal fibers) in 1906 after performing an autopsy on the brain of a fifty-one-year old woman afflicted with "dementia." Today, with the advent of neuro-imaging devices, scientists have also identified groups of degenerated nerve endings ("plaques") in Alzheimer's patients. The more plaques and tangles a patient has, the greater the intellectual and memory disturbance. Some scientists speculate that the plaques made of a protein called beta amyloid may be the result of a specific protein imbalance. Although, there is no single laboratory test that can be done to diagnose Alzheimer's, researchers are working to develop diagnostic tools that may make screening more effective.

Most Alzheimer patients develop late onset (after age sixty-five); however, there is a rare early onset form which has been linked to a gene pair (type apo E-IV) on chromosomes twenty-one and fourteen. Having this fairly common gene pair (15 percent of the population does), however, does not mean you will definitely develop Alzheimer's. Some people never do and others develop it very late in life. Thus, scientists believe there are additional underlying causes of the disease. Potential causes being investigated include a "slow virus," the accumulation of toxic metals (especially aluminum) in the brain, brain damage from FREE RADICALS, a reaction to inflammation in the brain, and key chemical deficiencies in the brain which interrupt healthy cell-to-cell communication. For example, a striking reduction (up to 90 percent) of an enzyme called choline acetyltransferase, which is critical in the biosynthesis of ACETYLCHOLINE, has been identified in some Alzheimer's patients.

Memory loss can be symptomatic of many physical conditions including nutritional deficiencies, vascular disorders, abnormal thyroid function, infections, pernicious anemia, adverse drug reactions, tumors, abnormalities in the cerebrospinal fluid, and normal aging. If you have typical memory problems like forgetting where you put your glasses or what your neighbor's name is, or if you remember things after the fact and feel like you knew it all along, then you shouldn't worry. The type of forgetting characteristic of the early stage of Alzheimer's is more troublesome than this. If you can't remember that you wear glasses, or where you were ten minutes ago, or who the current President is, or your ability to function socially or mentally has been compromised, then you ought to seek the immediate advice of a physician you trust. Early diagnosis of Alzheimer's is important.

Although, a cure for Alzheimer's disease has yet to be found, scientists are developing multiple treatments that are offering more hope than ever before to patients and their families. At least seventeen drugs are in development. "We have come a long way in understanding some possible causes, abnormalities underlying the symptoms, and ways to slow the progression of the disease with promising drugs, hormones, and nutritional therapies," reports Dr. Jay Lombard, author of *The Brain Wellness Plan* (1997).

■ *Promising Treatments*

A great deal of energy has been invested over the past two decades in an effort to find effective treatments and preventions for the devastating effects of Alzheimer's (see also Chapter 6: a review of neuro-nutrients) The range of treatments are wide. Non-steroidal anti-inflammatory drugs, such as aspirin and ibuprofen, are being used successfully to reduce the swelling associated with the disease and to slow progression. And, even more effective anti-inflammatories are eminent.

In addition, two drugs, Tacrine™ or THA, FDA-approved in 1993, and Aricept™ (Donepezil), FDA-approved in 1996 are easing the symptoms of many Alzheimer patients. Both drugs have been shown to slow the progression of the disease and provide small but meaningful improvements in memory and cognitive ability in mild to moderate stages of the disease. They work by blocking the function of acetylcholinesterase which breaks down ACETYLCHOLINE allowing NEUROTRANSMITTERS to last longer during transmission.

Science is typically more concerned with understanding mechanisms than with appreciating personal meanings, but to fathom memory's fragile power we must pay attention to both.

—Daniel L. Schacter
Searching for Memory

A substance called Huperzine A, Hyperzine A, or Hep A, derived from a form of moss (Huperzia serrata), is also showing promise in the treatment of Alzheimer's. Chinese physicians have been using this substance for centuries (also an acetylcholinesterase inhibitor) as a remedy for inflammation, fever, and memory problems. It is widely available at health food stores and is currently receiving a great deal of attention.

In addition, a drug called CX-516 (Ampalex™)—from a new class of drugs called ampakines—is being studied for its ability to intensify a very abundant brain transmitter called AMPA-glutamate, a chemical that is necessary for neurons to communicate with one another. According to studies appearing in the *Journal of Experimental Neurology* (Jan. 1997), low doses of CX-516 enabled elderly volunteers ages sixty-five to seventy-three to score nearly as well as twenty-somethings on a diversity of memory tests.

The hormone estrogen has been used in the treatment of the disease, as well; albeit cautiously, as estrogen may possibly increase the risk of breast and uterine cancer. Several studies have suggested that post-menopausal women on hormone-replacement therapy were less likely to get Alzheimer's. And, studies dating back to 1979 have focused on the ability of estrogen to improve verbal memory and verbal IQ scores. From stimulating new DENDRITE branching on neurons and strengthening SYNAPSES where NEURONS communicate with one another to reducing harmful FREE RADICALS that contribute to plaque deposits, estrogen has a multiplicity of effects that offers much promise in the treatment of Alzheimer's.

Vitamin E may also help slow memory decline in Alzheimer's patients. Dr. Leon Thal, director of the University of California, San Diego's Alzheimer's Disease Cooperative Study Center, found that patients who took high doses of vitamin E lived about eight months longer, or took about that much longer to become institutionalized or to progress to severe functional decline, compared with patients who received a placebo. Vitamin E, like estrogen, is believed to mop up cell-damaging free radicals that may be generated by the characteristic Alzheimer's plaques. To review other memory-related treatments and nutritional findings, please refer back to Chapter 6: Nature's Own Memory Nutrients.

◼ *Amnesia: Memory Gaps, Cracks, and Holes*

Amnesia—either partial or total loss of memory—can be caused by various conditions. These include head injury, medial temporal deterioration caused by disease (i.e., Alzheimer's, Korsakoff's syndrome), encephalitis (infection in the brain), a brain tumor, stroke, or certain types of mental illness for which there is no apparent physical damage. Alzheimer's disease, however, is the most common cause of amnesia. Various

Various forms of amnesia result in different kinds of memory loss, but the most common forms of amnesia are anterograde where post-trauma memory is lost, and retrograde where pre-trauma memory is lost. In some cases, a patient experiences both types called global amnesia.

forms of the condition result in different kinds of memory loss, but the most common forms of amnesia are anterograde where post-trauma memory is lost, and retrograde where pre-trauma memory is lost. In some cases, a patient experiences both types called global amnesia. Another form of amnesia, albeit uncommon, is called transient global amnesia. This condition can leave a gap in memory of a few seconds to a few hours without loss of consciousness or other impairment in an otherwise healthy middle-aged individual. It is believed that transient global amnesia may be caused by a temporary reduction in blood supply to certain brain areas, sometimes preceding an impending stroke.

Scientists learned a great deal about amnesia in the wake of a series of famous landmark operations conducted by Wilder Penfield and Associates on epileptic patients during the mid-1950s. When the surgeons removed an apple-sized chunk of the medial TEMPORAL LOBE in ten epileptic patients in order to reduce their seizures, the results were devastating. Although they were successful in lessening the seizures, normal memory function was lost in eight of the ten patients. One of these patients, known in subsequent scientific literature as HM, was virtually unable to form new memories post-operatively (anterograde amnesia). His memories prior to the operation, however, remained intact, and he was able to demonstrate some procedural memory (motor learning), but he could not remember who the president of the United States was (semantic memory), nor that he had just celebrated his birthday with his wife twenty minutes previously (episodic). These cases provided scientists with the knowledge that removal of both the HIPPOCAMPUS and AMYGDALA result in amnesia; however, if only one of these structures is removed, memory functioning remains intact.

■ *Red Flags for Your Memory: Take Notice!*

Although everyone forgets things occasionally, if two or more of the following more serious symptoms apply to you, seek the advice of your physician.

- **You can't remember where you were 10 minutes ago.**
- **You can't say what the top news story is this week, or remember whether you read the newspaper yesterday.**
- **You can't say who the president is.**
- **You have trouble articulating complex ideas.**
- **Your vocabulary isn't as rich as it used to be.**
- **You have difficulty dressing.**
- **You forget appointments; and can't remember your schedule.**

- You're irritable and easily frustrated.

- You've become paranoid, or have lost some emotional control.

- Your family has concerns about you, or you realize you have problems that are lessening your ability to function at work or socially.

Source: Emory University School of Medicine, Alzheimer's Disease Clinical Core

■ *Yellow Flags for Your Memory: Beware!*

Less serious symptoms of forgetfulness, like where you left your glasses or a tendency to repeat yourself, are often a result of being:

- Interrupted
- Distracted
- Rushed
- Stressed
- Confused
- Upset
- Excited
- Alarmed

- Enraged
- Physically tired
- Mentally drained
- Over-medicated or a side-effect of certain drugs
- On auto-pilot or not mindful
- Over-worked
- Under the influence of drugs or alcohol

■ *Green Flags for Your Memory:Reduce the Risk!*

Improve general forgetfulness with the following tips offered by, among others, B.F. Skinner who delivered a lecture called "Intellectual Management in Later Years" to The American Psychological Association at the youthful age of seventy-eight.

- Don't procrastinate; do it now.

- Practice being one-track minded.

- Organize yourself.

- Visualize what you want to remember.

- Take mental pictures of reference points and landmarks.

- Use image associations and linking techniques.

- Use proximity and context cues (i.e., retrace your steps).

- Pause when you want to remember something.

- Relax and get plenty of rest.

- Eat foods rich in neuro-nutrients (see Chapter 6).

- Take memory supplements.

- Develop good observation skills.
- Write yourself notes and use external memory aids.
- Rehearse things in your head.
- Establish a pattern (i.e., always hang your keys on the hook by the door).
- Keep your brain well oxygenated by drinking a lot of water and exercising regularly.
- Expose yourself to novelty, change, and challenges regularly.
- Seek feedback from others.
- Play games that emphasize thinking and remembering.
- Practice remembering.

Memory Booster
A Stroll Down Memory Lane

Everyone enjoys taking a stroll down "Memory Lane" from time to time. Consider the following prompts as you recollect in your Memory Journal some of the events and turning points of your childhood years.

- **Did you have an imaginary friend as a young child? What was his or her name?**

- **What was one of your favorite movies as a youngster? Why do you think it made such an impact on you?**

- **What was the naughtiest thing you ever did? Did you get caught? What happened?**

- **Did you attend your high school prom or other big dance? With whom did you attend? What did you wear? What was your favorite song of the time?**

- **Did you have a favorite grandparent or relative? What do you remember most about them?**

- **What were some of the major turning points or landmark events in your life?**

If you continue your stroll down Memory Lane, adding additional rememberences as you think of them, before you know it, you'll have written your memoirs.

Chapter Recollections

- What is the biological explanation for memory subjectivity?

- What influences can cause memory distortion or "false" memories?

- How are emotional experiences encoded differently than non-emotional experiences?

- How and why might a memory become repressed?

- Is it possible to block out a traumatic memory totally and forever? What factors make the repression-recovery controversy difficult to explain?

- What is priming?

- What implications might priming have with regard to memory distortion and unconscious personal preferences?

- What factors influence how much our memory diminishes as we age?

- Alzheimer's disease and other traumatic conditions that result in severe memory loss wreak havoc on victims and their families. What experimental treatments are showing promise in the treatment of these conditions?

- What are the different types of amnesia? What are the causes of this condition?

- What situations or circumstances contribute to memory problems?

- What actions can we take to reduce forgetfulness?

- What signs may indicate more of a problem than normal forgetfulness?

All of us

are avid collectors of memories.

—Rebecca Rupp
Committed to Memory

35 All-Time Best Memory Strategies

1 Incorporate Regular Relaxation Techniques

One of the most effective ways to improve your memory may be to consciously relax all of your muscles right before learning something new, report researchers at Stanford University, School of Medicine. It seems that muscle relaxation reduces the amount of anxiety frequently felt by a person trying to learn something new. A group of thirty-nine men and women (ages 62 to 83), for example, volunteered for a memory-improvement program conducted by the researchers. The volunteers were divided into two groups. Members of one group were taught to relax their major muscle groups, while the other group was simply lectured about how to improve their attitude about aging before taking a three-hour memory-training course. Results of the experiment showed a 25 percent greater recall on new learning (names and faces) with the group that was instructed in relaxation techniques.

2 Play Classical Music

University of California, Irvine researchers, Dr. Frances Rauscher and Dr. Gordon Shaw, demonstrated in experiments conducted in the early 1990s that people exposed to classical music—especially Mozart—displayed significant boosts in spatial-temporal reasoning abilities. This discovery, quickly dubbed "The Mozart Effect," has stimulated huge interest around the world. Some scholars, including Don Campbell, author of the book *The Mozart Effect*, believe that listening to classical music may also aid memory and learning; however, this premise has yet to be proven empirically.

3 Capitalize on the Power of Storytelling

Our semantic memory lives in the world of words. It's activated by associations, similarities, or contrasts. Stories provide a schemata or script for us to tag or anchor information to in our memory. Concrete images engage our emotions and sense of meaningfulness providing a context and cue for the new information. This may help explain why people remember the name of a new acquaintance better if provided after a few minutes of verbal exchange—that is, a "story" (or association) has had a chance to take form. Storytelling has long been a tradition of ancient cultures for passing on "memory" from one generation to the next. An American Indian tradition of tying a knot in a "memory rope" to honor a particular occasion provides a concrete reminder of important "marker" events. Other cultures collect mementos, write their memoirs, or create scrapbooks to help them remember.

When the oldest cask is opened,
And the largest lamp is lit;
With weeping and with laughter
Still is the story told,
How well Horatius kept the bridge
In the brave days of old.

—Lord Macaulay

4 Rely on Mnemonic Strategies Every Day

Get in the habit of using MNEMONIC tools on a regular basis. Encoding your memory in a systematic way from the outset is the best way to ensure you'll remember something. Research shows that people who use mnemonics learn two to three times as much as those who rely on their normal learning habits.

5 Write Down What You Want to Remember in Detail

For eons, diaries, logs, journals, and transcripts have been recognized as great external aids for ensuring accurate memory. Writing down an account of an experience immediately afterwards is the best way to remember it in detail. Bank tellers are trained to do this immediately following a burglary—even before they provide a police report, since memory distortion can occur, for example, simply by how an officer poses a question or by an overheard comment. Ship captains are required by maritime law to keep an official voyage log book. Courts, medical doctors, and therapists are legally required to record events, as well. Beyond leaving an uncontaminated record, the very act of writing, itself, improves your memory. This is why it is helpful to write or rewrite study notes and summarize a topic in your own words.

6 Organize Your Thinking

Imposing a physical order on information or providing a logical framework for it makes it easier to remember. If you wish to remember all mammals indigenous to South America, for example, group them by color, habitat, size, the letter they begin with, or order in the food chain. Organizing information makes it more manageable for the brain by providing an immediate reference point for its retrieval.

7 Use Movement to Engage the Body/Mind System

Movement reinforces your memory by providing an anchor or external stimulus to match the internal stimulus. If you want to remember that "hola" means hello in Spanish, touch your mouth with the tips of your fingers (like the Italian gesture for good) and say "Ooh-la-la." You have just associated a known physical gesture with a new word. When you repeat the movement, you will remember the word. Recent research suggests that two areas of the brain once thought solely associated with control of muscle movement—the BASAL GANGLIA and the CEREBELLUM—are also important in coordinating thought. Movement triggers memory just as taste, smell, and sight does.

8 Maintain Good Health Patterns

Compromised health, including minor conditions like a cold or high-blood pressure can hinder your memory. One study found that over a twenty-five-year period, men with hypertension lost twice as much cognitive ability as those with normal blood pressure. On the other side of the coin, a University of Southern California study found that people in their seventies were less likely to experience cognitive decline during a three-year period if they  stayed physically active. Adequate sleep, nutrition, and mental enrichment are key players in a healthy mind/body/memory lifestyle.

9 When Your Memory Escapes You, Probe It

You can probe for a "lost" memory by retracing your steps, running through the alphabet to see if a letter prompts a cue, recapturing the mood you were in when the memory was formed, or simply thinking about the context of the memory you're trying to retrieve.

10 Use Linking Strategies

To remember items on a list, link them with an imaginary action. For example, visualize them crashing together, getting stuck, or befriending each other. Place items underneath, over, inside, or beside one another. Have them dancing, talking, or playing together. Even the ancients recognized the importance of linking information in ways that used both imagination *and* order—long before we had objective evidence that the left side of the brain remembers in a sequential fashion, while the right side remembers color, rhythm, dimensions, and abstractions. The links can be funny, unreal, or ridiculous; they do not have to be realistic or reasonable. However, you will recall a concrete, action-oriented association better than an abstract one.

11 Challenge Yourself

The brain produces chemicals called NEUROTRANSMITTERS which carry messages between cells involved in recall and strategy-making. The availability of such neurotransmitters—including the memory-building chemical ACETYLCHOLINE—appear to increase in brains which are frequently used to meet problem-solving challenges. Landmark studies conducted in the late 1960s by Dr. Marian Diamond and colleagues at the University of California, Berkeley demonstrated that mice provided with an enriched environment developed more complex DENDRITIC branching than unchallenged mice. Perhaps, this is why people with high IQs often score higher on memory tests: They have more "memory links" or related neural circuitry available to build on—demonstrating the snowball effect of memory and enriched environments.

12 Get Adequate Sleep

Lack of sleep, especially during the dreaming phase (REM), may reduce a person's ability to remember complex learning. Research at the University de Lille in France indicates that the mind actually depends on sleep to retain difficult memory tasks. Dreams may, in fact, serve as a reinforcement for learning and recall; as well as a means for processing emotions—sorting the chaff from the grain—and eliminating the unnecessary information from your busy memory circuits. Some scientists report that even cutting your normal night's sleep by as little as two hours may impair your ability to remember things the next day.

13 Take a Multiple Vitamin Supplement

The recommended dietary allowances (RDA) or minimum guideline for good nutrition was established by analyzing disease states, not optimal mental functioning, notes Dr. Vernon Mark, President of Boston's Center for Memory Impairment and Neuro-Behavior Disorders. Many nutritionists, health-care professionals, and scientists advocate the supplementation of a healthy well-balanced diet with a nutritional supplement. Special attention ought to be given to the entire group of B vitamins since they are involved in maintaining a healthy brain-immune connection and impact mental energy; as well as Vitamin C, which aids in the production of memory-important NEUROTRANS-MITTERS. A study of 260 Albuquerque residents over the age of sixty demonstrated the effect of nutrition on memory. Those who had the lowest intakes of various nutrients (including vitamins C and B-complex) consistently scored lower on a memory test. A study of "healthy" British school children found that giving a simple multi-vitamin over an eight-month period increased nonverbal IQ by almost ten points. Nutritional deficiencies can be subtle and, thus, go easily undetected.

14 Eat Light, Eat Right, and Drink Plenty of Water

Choose low-fat, low-calorie meals. Scientists found that people given a mental skills test after they'd eaten a heavy meal totaling 1,000 calories made 40 percent more errors than a group of people who had eaten a light three-hundred-calorie lunch. Foods that are low in fat and high in protein are chicken (without the skin), fish, shellfish, veal, and lean beef. Low-fat vegetable protein sources include dried peas and beans; low-fat dairy products include low-fat cottage cheese, skim milk, and

soy-based foods. As more and more links are drawn between our moods and the foods we eat, we can't over emphasize the importance of learning about nutrition and its impact on brain functioning. Drinking plenty of water aids digestion, assists breathing, increases the oxygen carrying capacity of your blood, and maintains cellular health.

15 Consider Taking Memory Supplements

Advances in brain biochemistry have made memory supplements an effective approach to enhancing mental functioning. There are currently over one-hundred neuro-enhancers on the market or in trial phase. Many are available at health food stores nationwide. Phosphatidyl choline, phosphatidyl serine, and phenylalanine are primary ingredients in memory supplements and have been shown to play an important role in learning and memory (see Chapter 6: Nature's Own Memory Nutrients).

16 Expose Yourself to Novel Stimuli

Studies have shown that people remember things better that are new to their senses. Unfamiliar stimuli may trigger the release of memory-enhancing neurotransmitters that serve as a fixative for your memory.

17 Engage Your Emotions

Emotions get a privileged treatment in our brain's memory system. Studies suggest enhanced memory for events associated with emotional arousal. Negative emotions seem to be most easily recalled, but all emotionally-laden experiences are more easily recalled than neutral experiences.

I can't memorize the words by themselves; I have to memorize the feelings.

—Marilyn Monroe

18 Chunk Information, Especially Numbers

Random bits of information are easier to remember when broken down into meaningful patterns. For example, telephone numbers, social security numbers, and checking account numbers are all chunked into three and four digit subsets for this reason. Wasn't it easier to remember license plates in the "good old days" when they were simply three letters and three numbers with a space between them?

19 Use Rhymes, Acronyms, and Acrostics

As illustrated in the following examples, our memory loves prompts: *Rhymes* - Forget and be blue: We tied the knot in '82; or "Red, Right, Return" reminds sailors to keep red buoys on their starboard side when returning to port. *Acronyms* - HOMES provides a cue for the names of The Great Lakes: Huron, Ontario, Michigan, Erie, and Superior; *Acrostics* - King Philip Came Over For Ginger Snaps prompts us that plants and animals are classified by their Kingdom, Phylum, Class, Order, Family, Genus, and Species.

20 Capitalize on State-Dependent Memory

What you learn in one state of mind or external circumstance, you will best recall in a similar one. Thus, if you drink coffee while studying for a test, be prepared to drink coffee while you're taking it. In like fashion, sad events are more easily remembered when you're in a blue mood; and happy events are more easily remembered when you're in a cheerful mood.

21 Use Your Preferred Memory Modality

Determine what your learning/memory modality preference is and capitalize on it. Visual learners benefit from writing outlines and drawing mind-maps; auditory learners benefit from talking about the learning and creating rhymes and jingles. We are all kinesthetic learners, which means that our quality of memory will increase as we "touch" and handle things. Thus, experiments, real-life experiences, excursions, movement, and art are extremely beneficial to the memory process.

22 Interact With Material to Enhance Meaning

Instill meaning in information you wish to remember by finding a relationship between new and prior learning. Make a personal judgment about it, and you dramatically increase your chances of remembering it. Summarize it, restate it, ask questions about it, draw it, highlight it, act it out, sing it, write a joke about it, mind-map it, manipulate it, and discuss it.

23 Develop Acute Sensory Awareness

Most of the great memory performers and mnemonists in the world exhibit (or exhibited) exceptional sensory perception or sensitivity. Practice your own precise observation skills (as described in Chapter 5), and learn to pay better attention by tuning in all of your senses. Blank looking or hearing instead of real seeing or listening is a primary cause of poor memory. When you want to remember something, pause for a moment, tune in, and note (internally or externally) what you want to recall about the experience.

24 Develop a Positive Mental Attitude

Replace negative attitudes or self-criticism like, "I'm getting too old to remember things like this," to affirming ones like, "If I apply a mnemonic to this information, I bet I can remember it." Examine your self doubts and mental blocks. Most of them were probably established very young with no real or productive basis.

25 Practice Immediate Action

Train yourself to do things when you remember them. If you want to remember to make a phone call, do it now. If that's impossible, give yourself a physical prompt—leave a message on your home answering machine, write a note, or leave your cell phone in a prominent place.

26 Do Interval Reviews

Information that is reviewed one hour, one day, one week, and one month after initial learning will be remembered. The more exposure over time to a concept or skill, the more firmly it will be embedded in your memory. The old adage "practice makes perfect" underscores the body's need for feedback and correction in the learning process. Make frequent reviews part of your regular learning routine.

27 Give Your Brain a Shot of Glucose

Glucose, one of three *simple* sugars (other two are fructose and galactose) is the primary source of energy for the brain. If glucose is not available in the bloodstream, your brain cannot operate at peak efficiency. Some studies have concluded that eating sugar during or shortly after new learning improves recall of the new material. More specifically, it is the glucose that is a component of sugar that delivers this benefit. The danger, however, is in eating too much sugar. Some research has linked high-sugar diets to hyperactivity and learning disorders in children; and to obesity and other health problems in adults. Diet beverages that contain aspartame (marketed as NutraSweet™, Equal™, and Spoonful™), should **not,** however, be encouraged as a substitute. Many problematic health conditions, including memory loss, may be linked to the consumption of this chemical additive. It may be especially dangerous for diabetics and pregnant or lactating women and their babies. A newly FDA-approved sweet food (not an additive) called Stevia™, however, has no known side-effects and actually aids in the metabolism of sugar. The best way to derive the benefit of sugar in your diet is to eat a carbohydrate snack for quick energy when you need it: Crackers, a candy bar, or a soda (as long as it's not a diet soda) are adequate sources. Fructose (derived from fruit) is less effective as a mental energy sugar source, as it cannot cross the BLOOD BRAIN BARRIER directly.

28 Engage in Regular Exercise

Beyond increasing your physical strength, regular exercise helps keep your memory functioning by ensuring a healthy supply of blood and oxygen to the brain. It also stimulates a healthy release of endorphins—pleasure-providing NEUROTRANSMITTERS—which increase cheerfulness, a precursor for optimal learning and retention. In addition, studies suggest that exercise may also boost the body's production of BRAIN-DERIVED NEUROTROPHIC FACTOR (BDNF)—one of at least eight human-growth factors being studied for their possible role in increased learning capacity and cell protection from diseases such as Alzheimer's, Parkinsons, and Lou Gehrig's.

29 Avoid Sedatives and Substances That Induce Drowsiness

Anything that sedates the brain, including alcohol, benzodiazepines (used to treat anxiety), and many "recreational" drugs, stops your brain and memory from working at peak efficiency. If you want to relax, eat a high-carbohydrate food which stimulates tryptophan production and acts as a natural sedative.

30 Remember the BEM Principle

Pay extra attention to information presented in the middle of a learning session as the natural tendency of the brain is to remember what's presented in the beginning and end. In simple experiments, this natural bias is evident. Try it yourself. Give a friend a list of twenty words arranged vertically and ask them to try and remember as many as they can. When you subsequently quiz them, notice how many of the words they forgot were positioned in the middle of the column.

31 Become Aware of Your Ultradian Rhythms

Our mind and body operate on a basic ninety- to one hundred and twenty-minute rest-activity cycle known as an ultradian rhythm. Our mental performance, as well as other functions like dreaming, stress control, brain-hemisphere dominance, and immune system activity, are directly linked to this basic cycle. To enhance our memory performance, we must pay attention to the swings in our ultradian rhythms. Demanding tasks should be approached when you're on the upswing; whereby less mentally or physically demanding tasks can be handled when you're on the downswing.

32 Use Whole-Brain Thinking Strategies

Engage right- and left-brain hemispheres: If you do simple tasks that engage only one brain hemisphere, attention span is low, says Dr. Jerre Levy of the University of Chicago. When there's enough complexity, novelty, or challenge, however, both hemispheres are sparked and optimal mental functioning is the result. When both brain hemispheres are synchronized and engaged, peak performance is more likely.

33 Use Your Active Imagination

Visualizing abstract information into concrete images is the basis for many MNEMONIC tools. One strategy that incorporates the use of your imagination is to take an imaginary snapshot of something you want to remember: Focus, snap, and say, "This memory's worth commemorating." Another imagination tool is to visualize soothing or desirable things to help you relax. A state of relaxed alertness is best for learning. Imagery has even been shown to change body chemistry and give us more body/mind control. Give your vivid imagination permission to create in ways that are fun, humorous, absurd, and surreal. These images will have staying power. Make them colorful, three-dimensional, moving, action-oriented, realistic, or strictly fictitious. Your imagination is uniquely yours: What comes to it is organic and, therefore, a powerful cue for retrieving the memory at a later time.

34 Use Loci Pegs

Associate what you want to remember with particular parts of your body or rooms in your house. Try it for yourself. Determine ten things you want to remember and associate the first one on the list with the top of your head. Move down to your eyes, nose, mouth, throat, chest, belly button, hips, thighs, etc. attaching a chunk of information to each loci peg with an imaginative association. When you want to remember a piece of information, your loci peg will trigger the memory.

35 Provide Your Brain With Downtime

Provide your brain with downtime: To function optimally, your brain needs downtime for memory consolidation. If you don't give your brain a break at regular intervals, you can continue to study, but it will likely be unproductive learning time. The downtime imperative varies in number and length depending on the complexity and novelty of the information, as well as the person's previous exposure to it. A good rule of thumb, however, is to take a three to ten-minute break after every ten to fifty minutes of learning.

Appendix

Answer Key

Crossword Puzzle Answers (from page 20):

Across	Down
2. short-term	1. working
4. reflexive	3. explicit
6. immediate perceptual	5. implicit
7. visual	8. semantic
10. auditory/verbal	9. procedural
11. episodic	13. long-term
12. flashbulb	
14. sensory	

Implicit Memory Retrieval Quiz Answers (from page 34):
1. red; 2. stars at bottom left; pound sign is at bottom right; 3. American books appear right side up; British books appear upside down; 4. look and see; 5. to reader's right; 6. Benjamin Franklin and Alexander Hamilton; 7. to reader's right; 8. five rows of six stars and four rows of five stars.

Stress Test Results (from pages 130 and 131):
The Life-Change Index Scale was developed by Dr. Holmes at the University of Washington School of Medicine and colleagues as a general guide for determining the likelihood of illness due to stress from recent life changes. Listed below are the score categories and the associated probability of illness during the next two years for individuals with scores in the higher ranges. The test is only meant to be a general assessment of change-associated stress: It is not definitive, as individuals vary widely in health patterns and their responses to stress. Nevertheless, if you score in the top two categories, this may be an excellent time to counter your high stress level with stress-reduction activities.

Score Categories

0-149	No significant problem
150-199	Mild life crisis level with a 37% chance of illness
200-299	Moderate life crisis level with a 51% chance of illness
300 or over	Major life crisis level with a 79% chance of illness

Glossary

Terms Related to Memory: Words that appear in all capitals are also included in this glossary.

AAMI (Age-Associated Memory Impairment) - General memory fuzziness experienced by many people over fifty. Recent studies suggest that people with AAMI symptoms are more likely to develop Alzheimer's Disease later in life.

Acetylcholine - A common NEUROTRANSMITTER involved particularly in long-term memory formation.

Acrostics - A MNEMONIC technique that incorporates a poem or series of lines in which certain letters in each line form a name, motto, etc.

ACTH - (Adrenocorticotropin Hormone) A substance released into the bloodstream by the pituitary gland in response to stress or intense emotions.

Adrenaline - A substance released by the adrenal gland into the bloodstream in response to danger. When it reaches your liver, it stimulates the release of glucose for rapid energy. Also known as EPINEPHRINE.

Amnesia - Partial or total loss of the ability to memorize or recall stored information.

Amygdala - An almond-shaped complex of related nuclei located within the LIMBIC SYSTEM or midbrain area. A critical processor for the senses, its primary function may be its responsibility for bringing emotional content to memory (see illustration in Chapter 1).

Antioxidants - Chemicals or nutrients that "scavenge," neutralize, or absorb FREE RADICALS.

Blood Brain Barrier - A protective filtering mechanism of the blood vessels of the brain that keeps out (or slows down) unsuitable substances from entering the brain.

Brain-Derived Neurotrophic Factor (BDNF) - A naturally occurring hormone that stimulates the growth of neurites (tiny projections of a growing neuron carrying information between cells). BDNF , just one type of human-growth factor that is being studied for its medical potential to restore function in the aging, BDNF is showing promise in the treatment of Parkinson's and Alzheimer's diseases.

Cerebral Cortex - The outermost neuron-packed layer of the CEREBRUM about 1/4 inch thick and home of the most lofty abilities in the brain. Divided into left and right hemispheres and four distinct lobes, each of these regions specializes in different tasks—especially related to the diffuse storing of memories (see illustration in Chapter 1).

Cerebrum - The largest part of the brain, composed of the left and right hemisphere and divided by four lobes: FRONTAL, PARIETAL, TEMPORAL, and OCCIPITAL LOBE(S) (see illustration in Chapter 1).

Chunking - A MNEMONIC technique whereby a piece of information is broken down into number groups (or word groups) for ease in recall (i.e., a telephone number divided by a dash).

Cortisol-A type of corticosteroid made by the body's adrenal glands; and released in response to stress. Aids the metabolism of glucose, protein, and fats; and regulates the immune system.

Cryptomnesia - The human propensity to mistake the source of a memory or to "remember" something that really didn't happen. Meaning "hidden memory" in Greek, cryptomnesia happens to all of us to one degree or another, no matter how astute we think we are.

Dopamine - A powerful and common NEUROTRANSMITTER in the class of hormones known as Catecholamines. Involved in producing positive moods or feelings. It affects the nervous and cardiovascular systems, metabolic rate and body temperature; and is thought to play a role in controlling movements. Related to NOREPINEPHRINE.

Eidetic Memory - The ability to duplicate an exact image in memory (afterimage) enabling an individual to recall and describe it in detail shortly after looking at it. Also called photographic memory.

Encoding - A process by which sensory perceptions are electrochemically "sealed" or connected in the body through neuronal activity to form a potential memory.

Engram - The physical basis of memory (also known as a memory trace) believed to exist in a network of nerve cells as the result of the consolidation of memory. A unit of information encoded as a pattern of lowered resistance or increased conductance to electrical impulses resulting in an increased readiness to respond to NEUROTRANSMITTERS.

Epinephrine - See ADRENALINE.

Episodic Memory - Memories from past episodes in our personal lives.

False Memory - Any instance in which we remember things differently from the way they actually happened; or something or someone is falsely recognized.

Free Radicals - Molecules or molecular fragments that have an unpaired electron creating an unbalanced structure that is violently reactive.

Frontal Lobe(s) - One of four main areas of the CEREBRUM, the upper brain area, concerned with intellectual functioning, including thought processes, behavior, and memory (see illustration in Chapter 1).

Glucocorticoids - A group of steroids produced by the adrenal cortex that regulates the body's metabolism of carbohydrates, fats, and proteins; and affects the function of the central nervous system and immune response, among other things.

Glutamate - An amino acid found in every cell in the body; also used in the nervous system as a fast excitatory NEUROTRANSMITTER.

Hippocampus - A crescent-shaped structure located within the LIMBIC SYSTEM beneath the TEMPORAL LOBE that may be the site of learning ability; and also appears to consolidate information for storage as permanent memory (see illustration in Chapter 1).

Hypermnesia - The phenomenon of extreme or exceptional memory power exhibited by an individual.

Hypothalamus - A complex thermostat-like structure in the mid-brain area that influences and regulates appetite, hormone secretion, digestion, sexuality, circulation, emotions, and sleep.

Loci - An ancient mnemonic technique first recorded by Greek and Roman orators whereby a familiar set of locations is used to create visual images that give order to chunks of information one wishes to recall.

Long-Term Potentiation (LTP) - A model that explains the creation of memories as electrical stimulation which produces a long-lasting increase in the activity of synapses within the HIPPOCAMPUS (and possibly other brain regions). It suggests that SYNAPSES are altered by experience, allowing signals to travel more readily along this pathway once LTP has taken place.

Mild Cognitive Impairment (MCI) - Above average age-related memory impairment whereby other mental functions remain intact. May be a precursor stage to Alzheimer's. See also AGE-ASSOCIATED MEMORY DECLINE.

Mnemonics - A host of strategies and techniques designed to aid memory.

Multi-Tasking - The ability to perform several tasks at once or to switch back and forth rapidly between them. A decline in this ability is the chief memory problem among healthy older people.

Neurons - One of two types of brain cells: The second type is glial.

Neurotransmitters - Molecules that act as our brain's biochemical messengers relaying nerve signals between neurons. The correct balance of the more than 50 different types of neurotransmitters is responsible for proper mental functioning. Deficiencies can interfere with behavior, mood, and memory. Scientists postulate that the chemistry of our body is a critical element in the subsequent triggering of our recall.

Nootropics - Meaning literally "toward the mind": a class of drugs (usually pyrrolidone derivatives, like Piracetam) designed to improve learning and memory.

Noradrenaline - Another name for NOREPINEPHRINE.

Norepinephrine - A common NEUROTRANSMITTER in the class of catecholamines. Secreted by the adrenal gland, it is primarily involved in maintaining a constant blood pressure. It is also influences the fight or flight response, metabolic rate, body temperature, emotions, and mood. Closely related to EPINEPHRINE.

Occipital Lobe(s) - One of the four major areas of the upper brain located in the rear of the CEREBRUM and largely responsible for processing vision. Other three areas are PARIETAL, FRONTAL, and TEMPORAL LOBES (see illustration in Chapter 1).

Parietal Lobe(s) - One of the four major areas of the CEREBRUM located at the top of the upper brain and largely responsible for reception of sensory information from the body's opposite side. Also plays a part in reading, writing, language, and calculation. Other three lobes are OCCIPITAL, TEMPORAL, and FRONTAL (see illustration in Chapter 1).

Peptides (or Peptide Molecules) - A class of hormones that travel in the bloodstream. They consist of chains of amino acids and serve as information messengers for states, moods, thinking, and memory.

PET Scan (Positron Emission Tomography) - A computer imaging technique that allows scientists to view brain activity (or lack of it). A radioactive substance is introduced into the blood stream and tracked as energy is used in areas of the brain relative to the functions of thinking, memory, or emotional engagement.

Serotonin - A common NEUROTRANSMITTER most responsible for inducing relaxation and regulating mood and sleep. Antidepressants (like Prozac) usually suppress the absorption of serotonin making it more active.

Synapse - The junction whereby neurons communicate with other neurons in dendrite-to-axon contact stimulated by NEUROTRANSMITTERS.

Synesthesia - A rare condition (estimation: 1 person in every 500,000) whereby a person's sensory perceptions are involuntarily crosslinked. As such, they associate particular words, sounds, or objects with specific colors, tastes, or shapes often resulting in extreme-memory ability, but usually accompanied by difficulties in other areas of mental and social life.

Temporal Lobe(s) - A major structure in the CEREBRUM located in the middle of the upper brain near the ears and largely responsible for hearing, listening, language, learning, and memory storage. Other major areas include the FRONTAL, OCCIPITAL, and PARIETAL LOBES (see illustration in Chapter 1).

Thalamus - A key sensory relay station located deep within the mid-brain area (see illustration in Chapter 1).

Suggested Resources

10 Best Teaching Practice, 2nd Ed. (2005) by Donna Walker Tileston

12 Brain/Mind Learning Principles in Action (2005) by Renate Nummela Caine, Geoffrey Caine, Carol McClintic, and Karl Klimek

A Biological Brain in a Cultural Classroom, 2nd Ed. (2003) by Robert Sylvester

Becoming a "Wiz" at Brain-Based Teaching, 2nd Ed. (2006) by Marilee Sprenger

Brain Compatible Strategies, by Eric Jensen

Brain Fitness: Anti-Aging Strategies for Achieving Super Mind Power, by Robert Goldman, MD, PhD, Ronald Klatz, MD, DO, and Lisa Berger

Brain Matters: Translating Research Into Classroom Practice (ASCD)

(The) Brain Wellness Plan, by Jay Lombard & Carl Germano

Brain Workout, by Arthur Winter, MD and Ruth Winter, MS

Building Mental Muscle, by David Gamon & Allen Bragdon

Building the Reading Brain, PreK-3 (2004) by Patricia Wolfe and Pamela Nevills

(The) Care and Feeding of Your Brain, by Kenneth Giuffre, MD with Theresa Foy DiGeronimo

Classroom Activators: 64 Novel Ways to Energize Learners (2004) by Jerry Evanski

Committed to Memory, by Rebecca Rupp

Designing Brain-Compatible Learning, 3nd Ed. (2006) by Gayle Gregory and Terrence Parry

Don't Forget, by Danielle Lapp

Environments for Learning (2003) by Eric Jensen

Feeding the Brain: How Foods Affect Children, by C. Keith Conners

Graphic Organizers, by Karen Bromley, Linda Irwin De vitis, and Marcia Modlo

How the Brain Learns, 3rd Ed. (2006) by David A. Sousa

How to Explain a Brain (2005) by Robert Sylvester

Learning and Memory: The Brain in Action, by Marilee Sprenger (ASCD)

Managing Your Mind and Mood Through Food, by Judith Wurtman

Mega Memory, by Kevin Trudeau

Memory 101 for Educators, by Marilee Sprenger

Mindful Learning (2003) by Linda Campbell

Searching for Memory, by Daniel Schacter

Smart Drugs II: The Next Generation, by Ward Dean, MD, John Morgenthaler, and Steven Fowkes

Super-Memory: The Revolution, by Sheila Ostrander and Lynn Schroeder

Teaching Around the 4MAT Cycle, by Bernice McCarthy

Teaching with the Brain in Mind, by Eric Jensen

The Mind Map Book, by Tony Buzan

Your Memory, by Kenneth Higbee

Bibliography

Beaumont, J. (ed.). 1994. *Brain power*. London: Grange Books.

Birkmayer, G. 1996. Coenzyme nicotinamide adenine dinucleotide: new therapeutic approach for improving dementia of the Alzheimer type. *Annals of Clinical and Laboratory Science* 26: 1.

Bower, G. 1992. How might emotions affect learning? In *Handbook of emotion and memory: research and theory*. S. A. Christianson, (ed.) Hillsdale, NJ: Erlbaum.

Burchers, Sam, M. Burchers, and B. Burchers. 1997. *Vocabulary cartoons: learn hundreds of new SAT words fast with easy memory techniques*. Punta Gorda, FL: New Monic Books.

Burchers, Sam, M. Burchers, and B. Burchers. 1998. *Vocabulary cartoons: kids learn a word a minute and never forget it*, Punta Gorda, FL: New Monic Books.

Buzan, Tony. 1991. *Use your perfect memory*. New York: Penguin Books.

Chafetz, Michael. 1992. *Smart for life: how to improve your brain power at any age*. New York: Penguin Books.

Conners, C. Keith. 1989. *Feeding the brain*. New York: Plenum Press.

Conway, Martin A. (Ed). 1997. *Cognitive models of memory*. Cambridge, MA: MIT Press.

Crook, Thomas. 1998. *The memory cure*. New York: Pocket Books.

Dean, Ward, J. Morgethaler, and S.W. Fowkes. 1993. *Smart drugs II: the next generation*. Menlo Park, CA: Health Freedom Publishers.

Dragan, G.P., W. Wagner, E. Ploestenau. 1988. Studies concerning the ergogenic value of protein supplements and l-carnitine in elite junior cyclists. *Physiologie*, 25 (3): 129-132. (July/Sept).

Ebbinghaus, H. 1964. *Memory: A contribution to experimental psychology*. New York: Dover.

Fowkes, Steven W. 1996. Natural substances to make us smarter, *Nutrition & Healing*: March.

Fuster, Joaquin. 1995. *Memory in the cerebral cortex*. Cambridge, MA: MIT Press.

Galton, Sir Francis. 1909. *Memories of my life*. New York: Dutton Books.

Garfield, Patricia. 1975. *Creative dreaming*. New York: Simon & Schuster.

Gold, Paul E. 1995. Role of glucose in regulating the brain and cognition, *American Journal of Clinical Nutrition*. April, 61 (Supplement 4):987s-95s.

Goldman, Robert, Ronald Klatz, and Lisa Berger. 1999. *Brain fitness: anti-aging strategies for achieving super mind power*. New York: Doubleday.

Gordon, Patricia, and R. Snow. 1992. *Kids learn America: bringing geography to life with people, places, and history*. Charlotte, VT: Williamson Publishing Company.

Gottlieb, William (Ed). 1989. *Maximum brainpower*. Emmaus, PA: Rodale Press.

Greenfield, Susan (Ed). 1996. *The human mind explained*. New York: Henry Holt & Co.

Hannaford, Carla. 1995. *Smart moves*. Arlington, VI: Great Ocean Publishers.

Higbee, Kenneth. 1996. Y*our memory: how it works & how to improve it*. New York: Marlowe & Co.

Hobson, J. A. 1988. *The dreaming brain*. New York: Basic Books.

———1994. *Chemistry of conscious states*. Boston: Little Brown & Co.

Howard, Pierce. 1994. *The owner's manual for the brain*. Austin, TX: Leornian Press.

Hunt, Morton. 1983. *The universe within: a new science explores the human mind*. New York: Simon and Schuster.

Hutchison, Michael. 1994. *Mega brain power*. New York: Hyperion.

Jensen, Eric. 1998. *Teaching with the brain in mind*. Alexandria, VA: ASCD.

Lapp, Danielle. 1987. *Don't forget*. New York: Addison Wesley Publishing Company.

Levin, Edward, J. Rose, and L. Abood. 1995. Effects of nicotine dimethlaminoethyl esthers on working memory performance of rats in the radical-arm maze. *Pharmacology, Biochemistry, and Behavior*, 51, 2:369-73.

Leviton, Richard. 1995. *Brain builders*. Paramus, NJ: Prentice Hall.

Lino, A, M. Boccia, A.C. Rusconi, L. Bellomonte, and B.I. Cocuroccia. 1992. Psycho-functional changes in attention and learning under the action of L-acetylcarnitine in 17 young subjects: A pilot study of its use in mental deterioration. *Clin Ter* (Italy) 140 (June): 569-73.

Loftus, Elizabeth, and Geoffrey Loftus. 1980. On the permanence of stored information in the human brain. *American Psychologist* 35 (May):409-20.

Loftus, Elizabeth. 1980. *Memory*. Reading: MA: Addison-Wesley

Lombard, Jay, and C. Germano. 1997. *The brain wellness plan*. New York: Kensington Books.

Lorayne, Harry, and J. Lucas. 1974. *The memory book*. New York: Stein and Day Publishers.

Lyon, G. Reid, and Norman Krasnegor. 1996. *Attention, memory, and executive function*. Baltimore, MD: Paul H. Brookes Publishing Co.

Maguire, Jack. 1990. *Care & feeding of the brain*. New York: Doubleday.

Michaud, Ellen, and Russell Wild. 1991. *Boost your brain power*. Emmaus, PA: Rodale Press.

Neisser, Ulric. 1992. *Affect and accuracy in recall: studies of flashbulb memory*. Edited by Eugene Winograd and Ulric Neisser. New York: Cambridge University Press.

Netter, Frank. 1983. *The CIBA collection of medical illustrations: nervous system*. West Caldwell, NJ: CIBA-GEIGY Corporation.

Ostrander, Sheila, and Lynn Schroeder. 1991. *Super-memory: the revolution*. New York: Carroll & Graf Publishers.

Pelton, Ross, and Taffy Clarke Pelton. 1989. *Mind food & smart pills*. New York: Doubleday.

Ramachandran, V. S., and Sandra Blakeslee. 1998. *Phantoms in the brain*. New York: William Morrow & Co.

Reiser, Morton F. 1990. Basic Books. *Memory in mind and brain*. New York: BasicBooks.

Rose, Steven. 1992. *The making of memory*. New York: Bantam Doubleday Dell.

Rupp, Rebecca. 1998. *Committed to memory: how we remember and why we forget*. New York: Crown Publishers.

Schacter, Daniel L. 1996. *Searching for memory*. New York: BasicBooks.

Sheldrake, Rupert. 1988. *The presence of the past*. New York: Time Books.

Siegel, Daniel. 1999. *The developing mind: toward a neurobiology of interpersonal experience*. New York: The Guilford Press.

Trudeau, Kevin. 1995. *Mega memory*. New York: Quill William Morrow.

Tulving, Endel, and Daniel L. Schacter. 1990. Priming and human memory systems. *Science* 247: 301-306.

Turkington, Carol. 1996. *The brain encyclopedia*. New York: Facts On File, Inc.

Verny, Thomas. 1981. *The secret life of your unborn child*. New York: Summit Books.

Winter, Arthur, and Ruth Winter. 1997. *Brain workout*. New York: St. Martins Griffin.

Wurtman, Judith. 1988. *Managing your mind and mood through food*. New York: Harper & Row.

Index

About the Authors

A former teacher and current member of the International Society for Neuroscience, **Eric Jensen** has taught at all education levels, from elementary through university. In 1981 Jensen co-founded SuperCamp, the nation's first and largest brain-compatible learning program for teens, which now claims more than 25,000 graduates. He is currently President of Jensen Learning, Inc. in San Diego, California. His other books include: *Student Success Secrets*, *Teaching with the Brain in Mind*, *Brain-Based Learning*, *Brain-Compatible Strategies*, *Sizzle and Substance: Presenting With the Brain in Mind*, *Trainer's Bonanza*, *Completing the Puzzle*, and *Super Teaching*. He's listed in Who's Who Worldwide and remains deeply committed to making a positive, significant, and lasting difference in the way the world learns. Jensen is a sought-after conference speaker who consults and trains educators in the U.S. and abroad.

Karen Markowitz, MA, is a professional editor, freelance writer, and former educator who credits the research that went into this book with improving her memory. She has edited eight books on the brain and learning; and is charting new territory as co-author of *The Great Memory Book*. She lives with her family in Del Mar, California.

**CORWIN
PRESS**

The Corwin Press logo—a raven striding across an open book—represents the union of courage and learning. Corwin Press is committed to improving education for all learners by publishing books and other professional development resources for those serving the field of PreK–12 education. By providing practical, hands-on materials, Corwin Press continues to carry out the promise of its motto: **"Helping Educators Do Their Work Better."**